Integrated Chinese

中文听说读写

Simplified Character Edition
Workbook

Tao-chung Yao and Yuehua Liu
Yea-fen Chen, Liangyan Ge and Xiaojun Wang

Cheng & Tsui Company

First edition 1997
2003 Printing

Cheng & Tsui Company
25 West Street
Boston, MA 02111-1213 USA

Simplified Character Edition
ISBN 0-88727-265-7

Companion textbooks, character workbooks and audio tapes are also available from the publisher.

Printed in the United States of America

PUBLISHER'S NOTE

The Cheng & Tsui Company is pleased to announce the most recent addition to its Asian Language Series, *Integrated Chinese*. This entirely new course program for the beginning to advanced student of Mandarin Chinese will incorporate textbooks, workbooks, character workbooks, teaching aids, audio tapes, video tapes, CD-ROM computer programs and interactive multimedia programs. Field-tested since 1994, this series has been very well received. It is our intention to keep it a dynamic product by continuing to add, revise and refine the content as we get your valuable feedback.

This series seeks to train students in all four language skills: listening, speaking, reading and writing. It utilizes a variety of pedagogical approaches—grammar translation, audio-lingual, direct method, total physical response—to achieve the desired results. Because no two Chinese language programs are the same, *Integrated Chinese* provides those classes that cover the lessons more speedily with additional material in the form of Supplementary Vocabulary. The Supplementary Vocabulary section, however, is purely optional.

The *C&T Asian Language Series* is designed to publish and widely distribute quality language texts as they are completed by such leading institutions as the Beijing Language Institute, as well as other significant works in the field of Asian languages developed in the United States and elsewhere.

We welcome readers' comments and suggestions concerning the publications in this series. Please contact the following members of the Editorial Board:

Professor Shou-hsin Teng, Chief Editor
3 Coach Lane, Amherst, MA 01002

Dana Scott Bourgerie
Asian and Near Eastern Languages, Brigham Young University, Provo, UT 84602

Professor Samuel Cheung
Dept. of Oriental Languages, University of California, Berkeley, CA 94720

Professor Ying-che Li
Dept. of East Asian Languages, University of Hawaii, Honolulu, HI 96822

Professor Timothy Light
Office of the Provost, Western Michigan University, Kalamazoo, MI 49008

PREFACE

In designing *Integrated Chinese, Level One* workbook exercises, we strove to give equal emphasis to the students' listening, speaking, reading, and writing skills. There are different difficulty levels in order to provide variety and flexibility to suit different curriculum needs. Teachers should assign the exercises at their discretion; they should not feel pressured into using all of them and should feel free to use them out of sequence, if appropriate. Moreover, teachers can complement this workbook with their own exercises.

I. Listening Comprehension

All too often listening comprehension is sacrificed in a formal classroom setting because of time constraint. Students tend to focus their time and energies on the mastery of a few grammar points. This workbook tries to remedy this imbalance by including a substantial number of listening comprehension exercises.

There are two categories of listening exercises; both can be done on the students' own time or in the classroom. In either case, it is important to have the instructor review the students' answers for accuracy.

The first category of listening exercises consists of a tape recording of each lesson. For the exercises to be meaningful, students should *first* study the vocabulary list, *then* listen to the recordings *before* attempting to read the texts. The questions are provided to help students' aural understanding of the texts and to test their reading comprehension.

The second category of listening exercises consists of a tape recording of three or more mini-dialogues or solo narrations. These exercises are designed to recycle the vocabulary and grammar points introduced in the new lesson. Some of the exercises are significantly more difficult since students are asked to choose among several possible answers. These exercises, therefore, should be assigned towards the end of a lesson, when the students have become familiar with the content of the texts.

II. Speaking Exercises

Here, too, there are two types of exercises. However, they are designed for different levels of proficiency within each lesson and should be assigned at the appropriate time. In the first type, to help students apply their newly-acquired vocabulary and grammatical understanding to meaningful communication, we ask concrete, personal questions related to their daily lives. These questions require a one or two sentence answer. By stringing together short questions and answers, students can construct their own mini-dialogues, practice in pairs or take turns asking or answering the questions.

Once they have gained confidence, students can progress to more difficult questions where they are invited to express opinions on a number of topics. Typically, these questions are abstract, so the students will gradually learn to express their opinions and give their answers in paragraph-length discourse. As the school year progresses, these types of questions should take up more class discussion time. Because this second type of speaking exercise is quite challenging, it should be attempted only *after* students are well-grounded in the grammar and vocabulary of a particular lesson. This is usually *not immediately* after completing the first part of the speaking exercises.

III. Reading Comprehension

There are three to four passages for reading comprehension in each lesson. The first passage—usually short and related to the lesson at hand—recycles vocabulary and grammar points.

The second passage consists of slightly modified authentic materials, such as print advertisements, announcements, school diplomas, newspaper articles, etc. This passage may contain some unfamiliar vocabulary. The purpose of these materials is to train students to scan for useful information and not to let the appearance of a few new words distract them from comprehending the "big picture." Here, the teacher has a particularly important role to play in easing the students' anxiety about unfamiliar vocabulary. Teachers should encourage the student to ask: What do I really need to look for in a job announcement, a personal ad, or movie listings? Students should refer frequently to the questions to help them decipher these materials and should resist looking up every new word in their dictionary.

IV. Writing and Grammar Exercises

A. Grammar and Usage

These drills and exercises are designed to solidify the students' grasp of important grammar points. Through brief exchanges, students answer questions using specific grammatical forms or are given sentences to complete. By providing context for these exercises, students gain a clearer understanding of the grammar points and will not treat them as simple mechanical repetition drills.

Towards the last quarter of the lessons, students are introduced to increasingly sophisticated and abstract vocabulary. Corresponding exercises help them to grasp the nuances of new words. For example, synonyms are a source of great difficulty, so exercises are provided to help students distinguish between them.

B. Translation

Translation has been a tool for language teaching throughout the ages, and positive student feedback confirms our belief that it continues to play an important role. The exercises we have devised serve to reinforce two primary areas: one, to get students to apply specific grammatical structures; two, to allow students to build on their ever-increasing vocabulary. Ultimately, our hope is that this dual-pronged approach will enable students to understand that it takes more than just literal translation to convey an idea in a foreign language.

C. Compositions

This is the culmination of the written exercises and is where students learn to express themselves in writing. Many of the topics overlap with those used in oral practice. We expect that students will find it easier to put in writing what they have already learned to express orally.

TABLE OF CONTENTS

PART TWO

I. Initials and Simple Finals:

Please fill in the blanks with appropriate initials or simple finals.

A.1. _b_ a   A.2. p _o_   A.3. _m_ u   A.4. l _i_

B.1. f _o_   B.2. n _a_   B.3. _t_ i   B.4. _b_ u

C.1. _t_ a   C.2. l _e_   C.3. l _ü_   C.4. _k_ u

D.1. _d_ u   D.2. t _e_   D.3. n _u_   D.4. n _ü_

E.1. _k_ e   E.2. _g_ u   E.3. _h_ a

F.1. g _e_   F.2. k _u_   F.3. h _e_

G.1. _q_ u   G.2. _j_ i   G.3. _x_ u

H.1. j _ü_   H.2. q _í_   H.3. x _í_

I.1. _c_ a   I.2. _z_ e   I.3. _s_ i   I.4. _z_ ü

J.1. _c_ u   J.2. c _e_   J.3. _z_ u   J.4. _s_ i

K.1. _z_ i   K.2. s _i_   K.3. _c_ a   K.4. q _u_

L.1. _z_ a   L.2. _j_ i   L.3. s _u_   L.4. _q_ u

M.1. c _í_   M.2. _q_ i   M.3. _sh_ u   M.4. _zh_ a

N.1. _sh_ u   N.2. r _u_   N.3. ch _i_   N.4. _r_ e

II. Tones:

Please listen to the tape and mark the correct tone marks.

A.1. hē   A.2. mà   A.3. pá   A.4. dǐ

B.1. nǚ   B.2. rè   B.3. chí   B.4. zhū

C.1. mǒ   C.2. qú   C.3. cā   C.4. sì

D.1. tú   D.2. fó   D.3. zé   D.4. jǔ

E.1. lǘ   E.2. bǔ   E.3. xī   E.4. shì

F.1. gū   F.2. sè   F.3. cí   F.4. kǔ

G.1. máng   G.2. quán   G.3. yuǎn   G.4. yuě

H.1. yǐ   H.2. ér   H.3. sān   H.4. sì

I.1. bā   I.2. qí   I.3. liǔ   I.4. wǔ

J.1. jiǔ   J.2. shí   J.3. tian   J.4. jīn

K.1. mǔ   K.2. shuǐ   K.3. huǒ   K.4. rén

L.1. yǔ   L.2. zhuāng   L.3. qún   L.4. zhōng

III. Compound Finals:

A. Please fill in the blanks with compound finals.

1.a. zh_ai_   1.b. t_an_   1.c. k_un_   1.d. j_iong_

2.a. x_un_   2.b. q_ie_   2.c. j_in_   2.d. d_uo_

3.a. x_ia_   3.b. zh_en_   3.c. t_ou_   3.d. g_ong_

4.a. sh_uai_   4.b. b_iao_   4.c. z_ei_   4.d. q_uan_

5.a. j_iu_   5.b. d_ian_   5.c. x_in_   5.d. ch_an_

6.a. zh_en_   6.b. l_in_   6.c. k_uai_   6.d. j_ia_

7.a. s_ui_   7.b. x_üe_   7.c. p_ao_   7.d. ch_ua_

B. Please fill in the blanks with compound finals and mark appropriate tone marks.

1.a. m_____   1.b. zh_____   1.c. sh_____   1.d. zh_____

2.a. sh_____   2.b. t_____   2.c. l_____   2.d. b_____

3.a. s_____   3.b. j_____   3.c. k_____   3.d. d_____

4.a. l_____   4.b. q_____   4.c. t_____   4.d. x_____

5.a. f_____   5.b. p_____   5.c. x_____   5.d. j_____

6.a. b_____   6.b. j_____   6.c. q_____   6.d. t_____

7.a. l_____   7.b. g_____   7.c. q_____   7.d. x_____

IV. Neutral Tones:

Please listen to the tape and mark the tone marks.

A.1. guanxi	A.2. kuzi	A.3. shifu	A.4. keqi
B.1. zhuozi	B.2. gaosu	B.3. shufu	B.4. women
C.1. gege	C.2. weizi	C.3. dongxi	C.4. yisi
D.1. nimen	D.2. shihou	D.3. chuqu	D.4. pengyou
E.1. meimei	E.2. xihuan	E.3. jiaozi	E.4. xiansheng
F.1. zenme	F.2. didi	F.3. erzi	F.4. xiexie
G.1. jiejie	G.2. mafan	G.3. bobo	G.4. yizi

V. Exercises for Initials, Finals, and Tones: Monosyllablic Words

Please transcribe what you hear into *pinyin* with tone marks.

A.1. _____	A.2. _____	A.3. _____	A.4. _____
B.1. _____	B.2. _____	B.3. _____	B.4. _____
C.1. _____	C.2. _____	C.3. _____	C.4. _____
D.1. _____	D.2. _____	D.3. _____	D.4. _____
E.1. _____	E.2. _____	E.3. _____	E.4. _____
F.1. _____	F.2. _____	F.3. _____	F.4. _____
G.1. _____	G.2. _____	G.3. _____	G.4. _____
H.1. _____	H.2. _____	H.3. _____	H.4. _____
I.1. _____	I.2. _____	I.3. _____	I.4. _____

VI. Exercises for Initials, Finals, and Tones: Bisyllabic Words

Please transcribe what you hear into *pinyin* with correct tone marks.

A.1. _____   A.2. _____   A.3. _____   A.4. _____

B.1. _____   B.2. _____   B.3. _____   B.4. _____

C.1. _____   C.2. _____   C.3. _____   C.4. _____

D.1. _____   D.2. _____   D.3. _____   D.4. _____

E.1. _____   E.2. _____   E.3. _____   E.4. _____

F.1. _____   F.2. _____   F.3. _____   F.4. _____

VII. Exercises for Initials, Finals, and Tones: Cities

Please read the following words and identify which cities they are.

Example: Mài'āmì   --->   <u>Miami</u>

1. Bōshìdùn   --->   <u>Washington</u>

2. Lúndūn   --->   <u>London</u>

3. Niǔyuē   --->   <u>New York</u>

4. Bālí   --->   <u>Bali</u>

5. Zhījiāgē   --->   <u>Chicago</u>

6. Běijīng   --->   <u>Beijing</u>

7. Luòshānjī   --->   _____

8. Duōlúnduō   --->   _____

9. Xīyǎtú   --->   _____

10. Wēinísī   --->   <u>Venice</u>

VIII. Exercises for Initials, Finals, and Tones: Celebrities
Please read the following words and identify which celebrities they are.

1. Mǎdānnà   --->   _Madonna_

2. Màikè Jiékèsēn   --->   _Michael Jackson_

3. Yīlìshābái Tàilè   --->   _Elizabeth Taylor_

4. Bābālā Sīcuìshān   --->   _Barbara Streisand_

5. Aòdàilì Hèběn   --->   _Audrey Hepburn_

6. Suǒfēiyǎ Luólán   --->   _Sofia Loren_

7. Mǎlìlián Mènglù   --->   _Marilyn Monroe_

IX. Exercises for Initials, Finals, and Tones: Countries
Please transcribe what you hear into *pinyin* with tone marks and identify what countries they are.

Example: <u>Rìběn</u>   --->   <u>Japan</u>

1. _____ ---> _____

2. _____ ---> _____

3. _____ ---> _____

4. _____ ---> _____

5. _____ ---> _____

6. _____ ---> _____

7. _____ ---> _____

8. _____ ---> _____

9. _____ ---> _____

10. _____ ---> _____

X. Exercises for Initials, Finals, and Tones: American Presidents

Please transcribe what you hear into *pinyin* with tone marks and identify which Amercian presidents they are.

1. _____ ---> _____

2. _____ ---> _____

3. _____ ---> _____

4. _____ ---> _____

5. _____ ---> _____

6. _____ ---> _____

7. _____ ---> _____

8. _____ ---> _____

9. _____ ---> _____

10. _____ ---> _____

Lesson One   Greetings

I. LISTENING COMPREHENSION

Section One (Listen to the tape for the textbook)

A. Dialogue I (Multiple choice)

(d) 1.What did the man say to the woman?
      a. What's your name?
      b. I'm Mr. Wang.
      c. Are you Miss Li?
      d. How do you do!

(b) 2. What is the woman's name?
      a. Wang Peng
      b. Li You
      c. Xing Li
      d. Jiao Li You

(a) 3. What is the man's name?
      a. Wang Peng
      b. Li You
      c. Xing Wang
      d. Jiao Wang Peng

B. Dialogue II (True/ False)
(T) 1. Miss Li is a student.
(F) 2. Mr. Wang is a teacher.
(F) 3. Mr. Wang is an American.
(F) 4. Miss Li is a Chinese.

Section Two (Listen to the tape for the workbook) (Multiple choice)
A. Dialogue I
(   ) These two people are _____.
      a. saying good-bye to each other
      b. asking each other's name
      c. greeting each other
      d. asking each other's nationality

B. Dialogue II
(   ) 1. The two speakers are most likely _____.
      a. brother and sister
      b. father and daughter
      c. old friends reuniting
      d. strangers getting acquainted

(   ) 2. Who are these two people? They are _____.
      a. Mr. Li and Miss You
      b. Mr. Li and Miss Li

    c. Mr. Wang and Miss You

    d. Mr. Wang and Miss Wang

C. Dialogue III

(   ) Which of the following is true?

    a. Both the man and the woman are Chinese.

    b. Both the man and the woman are American.

    c. The man is Chinese and the woman is American.

    d. The man is American and the woman is Chinese.

D. Dialogue IV

(   ) Which of the following is true?

    a. Both the man and the woman are teachers.

    b. Both the man and the woman are students.

    c. The man is a teacher and the woman is a student.

    d. The man is a student and the woman is a teacher.

II. SPEAKING EXERCISES

Section One (Answer the following questions in Chinese based on the dialogues)

A. Dialogue I

    1. How does Mr. Wang greet Miss Li in Chinese?

    2. What does Miss Li reply?

    3. How does Mr. Wang ask what Miss Li's surname is?

    4. What is Mr. Wang's given name?

    5. How does Mr. Wang ask what Miss Li's given name is?

    6. What is Miss Li's given name?

B. Dialogue II

    1. How does Miss Li ask whether Mr. Wang is a teacher or not?

    2. Is Mr. Wang a teacher?

    3. Is Miss Li a teacher?

    4. What is Mr. Wang's nationality?

    5. What is Miss Li's nationality?

Section Two

A. You meet a middle-aged Chinese person on campus. Try to ask politely in Chinese whether he/she is a teacher.

B. You meet a Chinese student on campus:

    1. Greet him/her in Chinese.

    2. Ask his/her name.

C. Introduce yourself in Chinese to a Chinese student. Tell him/her what your name is and whether you are a student.

D. You just met a foreign student who can speak Chinese.

    1. Ask him/her whether he/she is Chinese.

    2. Tell him/her that you are American.

III. READING COMPREHENSION

Section One

A. Give *pinyin* for the following Chinese phrases:

1. 你好 _nǐ hǎo_ 2. 贵姓 _guì xìng_ 3. 名字 _míngzi_

4. 小姐 _xiǎo jie_ 5. 老师 _lǎoshī_ 6. 中国人 _zhōng guó rén_

7. 学生 _xué sheng_ 8. 先生 _xiānsheng_ 9. 美国人 _Měi guó rén_

B. Match the questions on the left side with the appropriate replies on the right. Write down the letter in the parentheses.

(E) 1. 你好！   A. 是，我是老师。
(D) 2. 您贵姓？   B. 不，我是中国人。
(B) 3. 你是美国人吗？   C. 我也是学生。
(A) 4. 你是老师吗？   D. 我姓李。
(C) 5. 我是学生，你呢？   E. 你好！

C. Read the passage and answer the questions. (True/False)

王小姐是中国学生。李先生是美国老师。

Ms. Wang is a Chinese student. Mr. Li is an American teacher.

(T) 1. 王小姐姓王。
(F) 2. 王小姐是美国人。
(T) 3. 王小姐不是老师。
(T) 4. 李先生不是中国人。
(T) 5. 李先生是老师。

Section Two

Chinese Business Cards

Below are four real Chinese business cards. Circle all of the characters that you recognize, and underline the characters denoting family names.

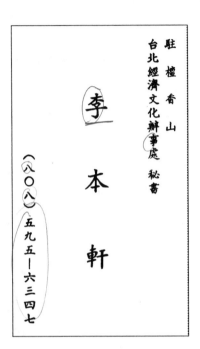

駐 檀 香 山
台 北 經 濟 文 化 辦 事 處　秘 書

李 本 軒

（八〇八）
五 九 五 — 六 三 四 七

美國夏威夷大學東亞語文系教授

李 英 哲
YINGCHE LI

EAST ASIAN LANGUAGES AND LITERATURES
UNIVERSITY OF HAWAII
HONOLULU, HAWAII 96822
U.S.A.

TEL : (808) 956-8406 (O)
FAX: (808) 956-9515
INTERNET : yli@aoc.lang.hawaii.edu

中 外 合 資
常州華潤裝飾工程有限公司
CHANGZHOU HUA RUN DECORATION ENGINEERING CO. LTD

王 德 中
WANG DE ZHONG
董事　副总经理

地址：中國常州勞動中路 42 號
ADD:№42 LAO DONG RD(M) CHANGZHOU
電話 TEL:8824743　8813361
傳真 FAX:0519 — 8824743
電挂 CABLE:5000　郵編 P.C:213001
宅電 HOME:6622599

台 北 美 國 學 校
外 語 系 中 文 部 主 任

王 智 寧

校 住 傳 電
址 宅 真 話
：： ／ ：
台 台 八 八
北 北 七 七
市 市 三 三
士 中 一 九
林 山 九 九
區 北 〇 〇
中 路 〇 〇
山 七 六 轉
北 段 114 二
路 巷 四 四
六 一 57 〇
段 一 號
八 四 三
〇 六 樓
號 九 一

IV. WRITING & GRAMMAR EXERCISES

Section One

A. Give the Chinese characters for the following sentences that are in *pinyin*.

1. Nín guì xìng?

您 贵 姓

2. Nǐ jiào shénme míngzi?

你 叫 什么 名字？

3. Qǐng wèn, nǐ shì xuésheng ma?

请问，你 是 先生 吗？

4. Wǒ shì Zhōngguórén. Nǐ ne?

我 是 中国人。你 呢？

5. Wǒ bú xìng Wáng, wǒ xìng Lǐ.

我 不 姓王，我 姓李。

6. Nín shì lǎoshī, wǒ shì xuésheng.

您 是 老师，我 是 先生。

7. Nǐ shì Měiguórén, wǒ yě shì Měiguórén.

你 是 美 国人，我 也 是 美 国人。

B. Rearrange the given Chinese words into a sentence, using the English sentence as a clue.

1. 叫 / 名字 / 你 / 请问 / 什么
   (May I ask what your name is?)

   请问你叫什么名字？

2. 姓 / 王 / 吗 / 你
   (Is your surname Wang?)

   你姓王吗？

3. 吗 / 是 / 你 / 学生 / 美国
   (Are you an American student?)

   你是美国学生吗？

4. 中国 / 是 / 人 / 我 / 不
   (I am not Chinese.)

   我不是中国人。

5. 小姐 / 先生 / 美国人 / 美国人 / 王 / 李 / 也 / 是 / 是
   (Miss Li is American. Mr. Wang is also American.)

   李小姐是美国人。王先生也是美国人。

C. Change the following statements into questions.

   Example: 我是学生。 ===> 你是学生吗？

1. 我是美国人。

   你是美国人吗？

2. 我姓李。

   你姓李吗？

3. 王老师是中国人。

   王老师是中国人吗？

4. 李小姐不是学生。

   李小姐不是学生吗？

Lesson Two   Family

I. LISTENING COMPREHENSION

Section One (Listen to the tape for the textbook)

A. Dialogue I (True/False)
(   ) 1. The picture in question belongs to Wang Peng.
(   ) 2. Little Gao doesn't have any younger brothers.
(   ) 3. Little Gao's parents are in the picture.
(   ) 4. All the people in the picture are members of Little Gao's family.
(   ) 5. Mr. Li does not have any sons.

B. Dialogue II (Multiple choice)
(   ) 1. How many people are there in Little Zhang's family?
     a. 3   b. 4   c. 5   d. 6

(   ) 2. How many people are there in Li You's family?
     a. 3   b. 4   c. 5   d. 6

(   ) 3. How many older sisters does Little Zhang have?
     a. 0   b. 1   c. 2   d. 3

(   ) 4. How many younger sisters does Li You have?
     a. 0   b. 1   c. 2   d. 3

(   ) 5. How many older brothers does Little Zhang have?
     a. 0   b. 1   c. 2   d. 3

(   ) 6. How many younger brothers does Little Zhang have?
     a. 0   b. 1   c. 2   d. 3

(   ) 7. How many children do Little Zhang's parents have?
     a. 2   b. 3   c. 4   d. 5

(   ) 8. How many sons do Li You's parents have?
     a. 0   b. 1   c. 2   d. 3

(   ) 9. Little Zhang's father is a _____.
     a. lawyer   b. teacher   c. doctor   d. student

(   ) 10. Li You's mother is a _____.
     a. lawyer   b. teacher   c. doctor   d. student

Section Two (Listen to the tape for the workbook) (Multiple choice)

A. Dialogue I

(B) Who are the people in the picture?
      a. The woman's father and mother.
      b. The woman's mother and younger sister.
      c. The woman's older sister and younger sister.
      d. The woman's mother and older sister.

B. Dialogue II

(C) 1. Which of the following is true?
      a. Both the man and the woman have older brothers.
      b. Both the man and the woman have younger brothers.
      c. The man has an older brother but no younger brother.
      d. The man has a younger brother but no older brother.

(C) 2. Why does the woman laugh at the end of the conversation? Because she finds it
      funny that _____.
      a. neither the man nor she herself has younger brothers
      b. neither the man nor she herself has older brothers
      c. the man has failed to count himself as his older brother's younger brother
      d. the man has failed to count himself as his younger brother's older brother

C. Dialogue III

(d) 1. The man's mother is a _____.
      a. teacher   b. student   c. doctor   d. lawyer

(a) 2. The woman's father is a _____.
      a. teacher   b. student   c. doctor   d. lawyer

D. Dialogue IV

(b) 1. How many brothers does the woman have?
      a. 1   b. 2   c. 3   d. 4

(d) 2. How many daughters do the woman's parents have?
      a. 1   b. 2   c. 3   d. 4

(C) 3. How many people in the woman's family are older than herself?
      a. 2   b. 3   c. 4   d. 5

(a) 4. How many people in the man's family are younger than himself?
      a. 0   b. 1   c. 2   d. 3

(d) 5. Why do the speakers disagree on the number of the people in the man's family?
      Because he forgot to count in _____.
      a. his older brother   b. his younger sister
      c. his younger brother   d. himself

II. SPEAKING EXERCISES

Section One (Answer the following questions in Chinese based on the dialogues)
A. Dialogue I

1. Whose photo is on the wall?
2. How many people are there in Little Gao's family? Who are they?
3. Is the boy in the picture Little Gao's younger brother? How do you know?
4. Is the girl in the picture Little Gao's younger sister? How do you know?

B. Dialogue II

1. How many people are there in Little Zhang's family?
2. How many children do Little Zhang's parents have?
3. What is the birth order of Little Zhang?
4. How many brothers and sisters does Li You have?
5. What is the occupation of Little Zhang's father?
6. What is the occupation of Little Zhang's mother and Li You's mother?
7. How many people are there in Li You's family?
8. How many daughters do Li You's parents have?

Section Two

A. Find a family picture and use this to introduce your family members to your friends.

B. Show your family photo to your partner and ask questions about each other's photo, such as: who the person is, if your partner has brothers or sisters, what each of his/her family members does.

C. Following are four members from Wang You's family. Please introduce them. Make sure that you mention what they do.

     1. Wang You's older brother.
     2. Wang You's mother.
     3. Wang You's father.
     4. Wang You's younger brother.

D. Introduce the family in the picture below. Please use as many new words as possible from this lesson.

III. READING COMPREHENSION

Section One

A. Match the questions on the left with the appropriate replies on the right. Write
   down the letter in the parentheses.

(B) 1. 这个人是谁？   *A.* 是我的。
Whose photo is this
(A) 2. 这张照片是谁的？   *B.* 这是我姐姐。

(E) 3. 你哥哥是学生吗？   *C.* 我家有五个人。
Nǐ jiā yǒu
(C) 4. 你家有几个人？   *D.* 我有两个弟弟。

(D) 5. 你有没有弟弟？   *E.* 我哥哥是医生。

B. This is a family portrait of the Gao family. Look at the photo carefully and identify
   each person.

1. 爸爸 (D)   2. 妹妹 (B)   3. 妈妈 (C)   4. 姐姐 (A)

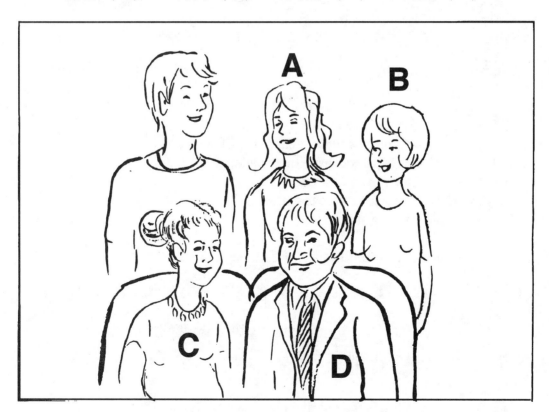

C. Give *pinyin* for the following Chinese words, and draw lines to connect the Chinese
   words and their English equivalents.

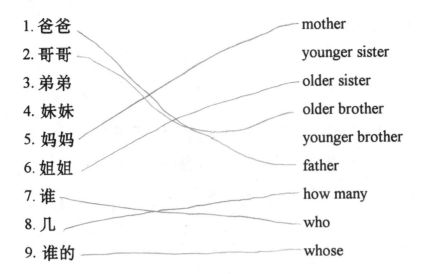

1. 爸爸 — father
2. 哥哥 — older brother
3. 弟弟 — younger brother
4. 妹妹 — younger sister
5. 妈妈 — mother
6. 姐姐 — older sister
7. 谁 — who
8. 几 — how many
9. 谁的 — whose

Section Two

A. Read the passage and answer the questions (True/False)

小高家有五个人，爸爸、妈妈、一个姐姐、一个妹妹和他。他的爸爸是医生，妈妈是律师，姐姐是老师，他和妹妹都是学生。

(T) 1. Little Gao has two sisters.
(F) 2. Little Gao has one brother.
(F) 3. Little Gao is the youngest child in his family.
(T) 4. Little Gao's parents have three children.
(F) 5. Little Gao's parents are doctors.
(F) 6. Little Gao's sisters are teachers.
(T) 7. Little Gao is a student.

B. Read the passage and answer the questions (True/False)

小王家有六个人。她的爸爸是老师，妈妈是医生。她有一个哥哥、两个妹妹。她的哥哥也是医生，她和两个妹妹都是学生。

(F) 1. Little Wang is the oldest child in the family.
(F) 2. Little Wang's father and her brother are both teachers.
(T) 3. Little Wang's parents have only one son.
(T) 4. Little Wang's mother and brother are both doctors.
(T) 5. All the girls in the Wang family are students.

IV. WRITING & GRAMMAR EXERCISES

Section One

A. Answer the following questions about yourself in complete sentences, using 有 or 没有. If the answer is positive, please state how many there are.

Examples: 1. *A:* 你有哥哥吗？ *B:* 我没有哥哥。

2. *A:* 你有哥哥吗？ *B:* 我有三个哥哥。

1. *A:* 你有姐姐吗？ *B:* 我有一个姐姐 。

2. *A:* 你有妹妹吗？ *B:* 我没有妹妹 。

3. *A:* 你有弟弟吗？ *B:* 我没有弟弟 。

4. *A:* 你有哥哥吗？ *B:* 我没有哥哥 。

B. Rewrite the following sentences using 都

Example: 小高是学生，王朋也是学生。

===> 小高、王朋都是学生。

1. 小高有姐姐，小张也有姐姐。

小高，小张都有姐姐。

2. 王朋是学生，李友也是学生。

王朋，李友 都是 学生。

3. 这张照片是你的，那张照片也是你的。

张照片 都是 你的。

4. 这个人姓李，那个人也姓李。

她们 都个人 姓李。

5. 李友没有我的照片，王朋也没有我的照片。

李友，王朋 都 没有 我的照片。

6. 他哥哥不是律师，他弟弟也不是律师。

他哥哥 ~~和~~ 弟 都不 ~~律师~~ 。
          是

7. 王朋有哥哥，小高有哥哥，李友没有哥哥。

王朋, 小高 都有哥哥。李友 没有哥哥。

8. 我爸爸是医生，我妈妈是医生，我哥哥是律师。

我爸爸, 妈妈 都是 医生。

C. Fill in the blanks with "这" or "那" based on the descriptions for each situation.

1. You point to a person standing about thirty feet away, and say:

   那 个人是我的老师，他是中国人。

2. You are holding a family photo in your hand, and say:

   这 是我爸爸， 这 是我妈妈。

3. You look down the hallway and recognize someone, and say:

   那 个医生叫李生一，是李友的爸爸。

4. You introduce to your friend a girl sitting at the same table, and say:

   这 是李先生的女儿。

D. Fill in the blanks with the appropriate question words. (什么、谁、谁的、几)

1. A: 谁的 名字叫王朋？   B: 他的名字叫王朋。

2. A: 李老师家有 几 个人？   B: 他家有三个人。

3. A: 你爸爸做 什么 ？   B: 我爸爸是医生。

4. A: 你妹妹叫 名字？   B: 我妹妹叫高美美。

5. A: 那个美国人是 谁 ？   B: 他叫David Smith，是我的老师。

6. A: 你有 几 张你妈妈的照片？   B: 我有两张。

E. Translate the following sentences into Chinese, using the words and phrases given in parentheses.

1. Little Wang, is this photograph yours?（是…吗？）

小王，这张照片是你的吗？

2. Mr. Zhang has three daughters.

张先生有三个女儿。

3. Mr. Wang has no sons.

王先生没有儿子。

4. Is this boy your older brother?

5. Is this girl your younger sister?

6. *A:* Who is this person?（谁）

这个人是谁？

B: She's my younger sister.（是）

她是我妹妹。

7. *A:* Is that your older brother?

B: No, he's my father.（不是）

8. *A:* Do you have any younger brothers?（有）

B: No, I don't have any younger brothers.（没有）

9. *A:* How many older sisters do you have?（有，几）

B: I have two older sisters.

10. How many people are there in your family?（有，几）

11. There are six people in my family: my dad, my mom, two older brothers, a
    younger sister and I.（有）

    hé wǒ.

12. *A:* What do your older brothers and older sisters do?（什么）

    Subject+verb+o

B: My older brothers and older sisters are all students.

13. *A:* My mom is a lawyer. My dad is a doctor. How about your mom and dad?
    （呢）

B: My mom is a lawyer, too. My dad is a teacher.（也）

14. Both my teacher and her teacher are Americans.

15. Neither Little Gao nor Little Zhang is Chinese.

Section Two

A. List your family members in Chinese.

爸爸，妈妈

B. To the best of your Chinese ability, tell what each of your family members does.

C. Please write a paragraph describing the picture below?

Some suggestions:

This is Little Zhang's picture. Little Zhang is my friend. He is Chinese.
He is a teacher. He has seven students

Lesson Three   Dates and Time

I. LISTENING COMPREHENSION

Section One (Listen to the tape for the textbook) (True/False)

A. Dialogue I

(   ) 1. Little Gao is eighteen years old.
(   ) 2. September 12 is Thursday.
(   ) 3. October 7 is Little Gao's birthday.
(   ) 4. Little Bai will treat Little Gao to a dinner on Thursday.
(   ) 5. Little Gao is American; therefore he likes American food.
(   ) 6. Little Bai refuses to eat American food.
(   ) 7. They will have dinner together at 6:30.

B. Dialogue II

(   ) 1. Wang Peng will not be free until 6:15.
(   ) 2. Wang Peng will not be busy tomorrow.
(   ) 3. Little Bai is inviting Wang Peng to dinner.
(   ) 4. Tomorrow is Little Bai's birthday.
(   ) 5. Wang Peng doesn't know Little Gao.
(   ) 6. Little Li is Little Bai's schoolmate.
(   ) 7. Wang Peng doesn't know Little Li.

Section Two (Listen to the tape for the workbook)

Dialogue I (Multiple choice)

(   ) 1. Today's date is _____.
　　　　　　 a. May 10　　　b. June 10　　　c. October 5　　d. October 6

(   ) 2. What day is today?
　　　　　　 a. Thursday　　b. Friday　　　c. Saturday　　d. Sunday

(   ) 3. What day is October 7? It is _____.
　　　　　　 a. Thursday　　b. Friday　　　c. Saturday　　d. Sunday

B. Dialogue II (True/False)

(   ) 1. Both speakers in the dialogue are Chinese.
(   ) 2. The man invites the woman to dinner because it will be his birthday tomorrow.
(   ) 3. The man likes Chinese food.
(   ) 4. The woman does not like Chinese food.

C. Dialogue III (True/False)

(   ) 1. Today the woman is busy.
(   ) 2. Today the man is not busy.
(   ) 3. Tomorrow both the man and the woman will be very busy.

33

D. Dialogue IV (Multiple choice)

(   ) 1. What time does the man propose to meet?
           a) 6:30   b) 7:00   c) 7:30   d) 8:00

(   ) 2. What time do they finally agree upon?
           a) 6:30   b) 7:00   c) 7:30   d) 8:00

(   ) 3. What day are they going to meet?
           a) Thursday
           b) Friday
           c) Saturday
           d) Sunday

II. SPEAKING EXERCISES

Section One (Answer the following questions in Chinese based on the dialogues)

A. Dialogue I
1. When is Little Gao's birthday?
2. How old is Little Gao?
3. Who is going to treat whom?
4. What is Little Gao's nationality?
5. What kind of dinner are they going to have?
6. What time is the dinner?

B. Dialogue II
1. Why does Little Bai ask if Wang Peng is busy or not?
2. When is Wang Peng busy?
3. Who else will go out for dinner tomorrow with Little Bai and Wang Peng?
4. Does Little Bai know Little Li? How do you know?

Section Two

A. Tomorrow is your partner's birthday. Find out how old he/she is and offer to take him/her out for dinner. Ask him/her if he/she prefers Chinese or American food and decide the time for the dinner.

B. Invite a mutual friend to join you and your partner for the dinner. Explain what the occasion is and who else will be there.

C. Your partner would like to take you out for dinner on your birthday, but you will be very busy on your birthday. Suggest another day for the dinner and decide the time for the dinner.

III. READING COMPREHENSION

Section One

A. Read the passages and answer the questions. (Multiple choice)

(d)1. 今天星期六，明天星期几？
- a. Thursday
- b. Friday
- c. Saturday
- d. Sunday

Thurs, October 2nd,   *October 4th is what day?*

(c)2. 十月二号星期四，十月四号星期几？

- a. 星期四
- b. 星期五
- c. 星期六
- d. 星期日

B. Write the following times in English.

1. 三点钟：___three o'clock___
2. 两点十分：___two ten minutes___
3. 六点五十分：___6:50___
4. 晚上八点钟：___20:00___
5. 晚上九点一刻：___21:15___
6. 晚上十一点半：___23:30___

C. Fill in the blanks in English below based on the calendar.

year + month + date + day

```
      1997年
         nián
     九　月
    22日  hào 号
     星期一
      星
  xīng qí  yí ~ Monday
```

Sunday ~ Tian
xīng qí

The date on this calendar is ___Monday, Sept. 22, 1997.___

The day of the week is ___Monday___.

Next month is ___October___.

The day after tomorrow is a ___Wednesday___.

Section Two

A. Read the passage and answer the questions. (True/False)

> 明天是小白的同学小高的生日。小白和他姐姐请小高吃饭，因为小白的姐姐也认识小高。小高是美国人，可是他喜欢吃中国饭。明天晚上他们吃中国饭。

(F) 1. Tomorrow is Little Bai's birthday.
(T) 2. Little Bai's sister knows Little Gao.
(T) 3. Little Gao and Little Bai are classmates.
(F) 4. Little Gao is Chinese.
(T) 5. Little Gao likes Chinese food.
(F) 6. Little Gao is going to pay for the dinner.

B. Read the passage and answer the questions. (True/False)

> 李小姐、白小姐和高先生是同学。今天是李小姐的生日，晚上六点半白小姐和高先生的妹妹请她吃晚饭，可是李小姐不认识高先生的妹妹。

(T) 1. Miss Li and Miss Bai are classmates.
(F) 2. Miss Li is going to treat Miss Bai to dinner tonight.
(T) 3. Today is Miss Li's birthday.
(T) 4. Miss Li will not have dinner at home this evening.
(F) 5. Miss Li will see Mr. Gao at 6: 30 p. m..
(F) 6. Miss Li and Mr. Gao's younger sister are close friends.

C. Which of the following is the correct way to say "June 3, 1997" in Chinese?

1. 六月三日一九九七年

2. 三日六月一九九七年

3. 六月一九九七年三日

4. 一九九七年六月三日

The correct answer is: ____4.____ .

IV. WRITING & GRAMMAR EXERCISES

Section One

A. Write the following numbers using Chinese characters.

    1. 15   十五

    2. 93   九十三

    3. 47   四十七

    4. 62   六十二

    5. your phone number   五

B. Turn the following dates or time phrases into Chinese and write down the Chinese version in characters.

    1. November 12   十一月 十二 日

    2. Friday evening   星期五 晚上

    3. 7:00 this evening   晚上 七点

    4. 8:30 p.m. Saturday   星期六 晚上 八点半

    5. quarter after nine   上 九点 一刻

C. Please complete the following exchanges.

    1. A: 今天是几月几号？   B: 十一月二十二日 。

    2. A: 你的生日是＿＿年＿＿？   B: 我的生日是 一九八三 年 。

    3. A: 你今年多大？   B: 我今年二十 。

    4. A: 现在几点钟？   B: 现在 八 点 三十五 分。

    5. A: 你几点 吃晚饭 ？   B: 我五点三刻吃晚饭。

D. Please complete the following questions using "A-not-A" form.
        Example: A: 王朋明天有没有事？
              B: 王朋明天没有事。

1. *A:* 王先生是不是中国人？_____ ?

   B: 王先生是中国人。

2. *A:* 小高有没有弟弟？_____ ?

   B: 小高没有弟弟。

3. *A:* 小高喜欢不喜欢吃美国饭_____ ?

   B: 小高喜欢吃美国饭。

4. *A:* 王朋明天忙不忙_____ ?

   B: 王朋明天不忙。

5. *A:* 小张是不是医生_____ ?

   B: 小张的爸爸不是医生。

E. Please complete the following questions with 还是 .
   Example: *A:* 王朋是中国人还是美国人？

   　　　B: 王朋是中国人。

1. *A:* 我喜欢吃美国饭还是中国饭_____ ?

   B: 我喜欢吃美国饭。

2. *A:* 小白是小高的同学还是朋友_____ ?

   B: 小白是小高的同学。

3. *A:* 小张的爸爸还是妈妈是律师_____ ?

   B: 小张的爸爸是律师。

4. *A:* 李友不是老师还是王朋不是老师_____ ?

   B: 李友不是老师。

5. *A:* 星期二还是星期五是我的生日_____ ?

   B: 星期二是我的生日。

Lesson Four   Hobbies

I. LISTENING COMPREHENSION

Section One (Listen to the tape for the textbook) (True/False)

A. Dialogue I

(T) 1. Little Gao likes watching T.V.
(F) 2. Little Bai does a lot of reading every weekend.
(T) 3. Little Bai likes not only singing, but also dancing.
(F) 4. Little Gao likes playing ball and listening to music on weekends.
(F) 5. Both Little Gao and Little Bai like dancing.
(F) 6. Little Bai is treating Little Gao to a movie.

B. Dialogue II

(T) 1. Little Zhang does not like playing ball.
(T) 2. Wang Peng wants to play ball this weekend.
(F) 3. Little Zhang is very interested in movies.
(F) 4. Wang Peng is going out to eat with Little Zhang.
(T) 5. Little Zhang likes to sleep.
(F) 6. In the end Wang Peng gives up the idea of going out with Little Zhang.

Section Two (Listen to the tape for the workbook)

Dialogue I (Multiple choice)

(b) 1. What will the man most likely do on weekends?
       a. go to concert   b. play ball
       c. go to the movies   d. go dancing

(a) 2. If the man and the woman decide to do something together over the weekend, they will most likely go to _____.
       a. a movie   b. a concert   c. a dance   d. a ball game

Dialogue II (True/False)

(T) 1. The woman doesn't like Chinese movies because her Chinese is not good enough.
(T) 2. The woman prefers American movies over Chinese movies.
(F) 3. The man invites the woman to an American movie at the end of the conversation.

Dialogue III (True/False)

(T) 1. The woman invites the man to a concert.
(T) 2. The man is interested in sports.
(F) 3. The man invites the woman to go dancing.

43

Dialogue IV (Multiple choice)

(b) 1. The man invites the woman to _____.
    a. a dinner   b. a movie
    c. a dance   d. a concert

(c) 2. The man gives the invitation because _____.
    a. the woman has invited him to a dinner before
    b. the woman has invited him to a concert before
    c. tomorrow is his birthday
    d. tomorrow is her birthday

(d) 3. Which of the following statements is true?
    a. The woman doesn't accept the invitation although she will not be busy tomorrow.
    b. The woman doesn't accept the invitation because she'll be busy tomorrow.
    c. The woman accepts the invitation although she'll be busy tomorrow.
    d. The woman accepts the invitation because she will not be busy tomorrow.

E. Narrative (Multiple choice)

(   ) 1. The speaker probably spends most of his spare time _____.
    a. in movie theaters   b. in concert halls
    c. in front of a TV set   d. in a library

(c) 2. According to the speaker, Wang Peng loves _____.
    a. movies and TV   b. dancing and books
    c. dancing and music   d. books only

(   ) 3. Which of the following statements is true about the speaker and Wang Peng?
    a. Wang Peng likes to read.
    b. The speaker likes to watch TV.
    c. Both the speaker and Wang Peng like to dance.
    d. Wang Peng and the speaker are classmates.

Which one on the left side is known as "dǎqiú" in Chinese?

II. SPEAKING EXERCISES

Section One (Answer the following questions in Chinese based on the dialogues)
A. Dialogue I
      1. What does Little Gao like to do on weekends?
      2. What does Little Bai like to do on weekends?
      3. What will Little Bai and Little Gao do tonight?
      4. Who is treating tonight?
      5. Who took whom to dinner yesterday?

B. Dialogue II
      1. Did Wang Peng see Little Zhang yesterday? How do you know?
      2. Does Little Zhang want to play ball? Why?
      3. Does Little Zhang want to go to the movies? Why?
      4. What does Little Zhang like to do?
      5. What did Wang Peng finally decide to do this weekend?

Section Two
A. Discuss your interests and hobbies with your friends, and then make an appointment with them based on your common interest.

B. Your partner is inviting you to do something. Keep rejecting the suggestions he/she gives and give reasons why you do not like those activities.

C. How do you say the following sports in Chinese?

III. READING COMPREHENSION

Section One

A. Match the phrases with the appropriate pictures.

(A) 1. 打球 (D) 2. 跳舞 (B) 3. 唱歌 (E) 4. 听音乐 (C) 5. 看电视

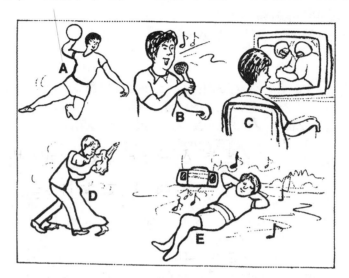

B. Match the questions on the left with the appropriate replies on the right. Write down the letter in the parentheses.

(　) 1. 你叫什么名字？   A. 我明天不忙。
(　) 2. 这是你弟弟吗？   B. 今天晚上我很忙。
(　) 3. 你明天忙不忙？   C. 我想看一个外国电影。
(　) 4. 你认识小张吗？   D. 不,这是我哥哥。
(　) 5. 你喜欢听音乐吗？   E. 因为我喜欢吃美国饭。
(J) 6. 为什么你请我看电影？   F. 认识,他是我同学。
(E) 7. 为什么我们不吃中国饭？   G. 我叫王朋。
(　) 8. 我们去打球,好吗？   H. 我觉得听音乐没有意思。
(　) 9. 这个周末你做什么？   I. 我不想打球。
(　) 10. 今天晚上我去找你,好吗？   J. 因为今天是你的生日。

Section Two

A. Read the passage and answer the questions. (True/False)

昨天是张律师的生日，他的同学王先生昨天晚上请他吃晚饭。因为王先生请张律师吃饭，所以张律师这个周末想请王先生去看一个外国电影。

(F) 1. Yesterday was Lawyer Wang's birthday.
(T) 2. Yesterday Lawyer Zhang didn't have dinner at home.
(F) 3. Yesterday Mr. Wang and Lawyer Zhang went to see a foreign movie.
(F) 4. Mr. Wang wants to take Lawyer Zhang to see a movie because Lawyer Zhang took him out for dinner.

B. Read the passage and answer the questions. (Multiple choice)

小王和小李是同学。小王是中国人，他喜欢打球、看电视和看书。小李是美国人，她喜欢听音乐、唱歌和跳舞。他们都喜欢看电影，可是小王只喜欢看美国电影，小李觉得美国电影没有什么意思，她只喜欢看外国电影。她觉得中国电影很有意思。

(d) 1. What does Little Wang like to do?
    a. Watching TV and listening to music
    b. Watching Chinese movies and dancing
    c. Watching American movies and singing
    d. Playing ball and reading

(b) 2. What does Little Li like to do?
    a. Watching TV and listening to music
    b. Watching Chinese movies and dancing
    c. Watching American movies and dancing
    d. Playing ball and reading

(d) 3. Which of the following statements is true?
    a. Little Wang and Little Li both like to watch TV.
    b. Little Wang is American and he likes American movies.
    c. Little Li is Chinese and she likes American movies.
    d. Little Wang and Little Li know each other.

(d) 4. If Little Wang and Little Li want to do something they are both interested in, where can they go together?
    a. A movie theater
    b. A library
    c. A dancing party
    d. None of the above

IV. WRITING & GRAMMAR EXERCISES

Section One

A. Use a word or phrase from each of the four following groups to make four sentences based on the Chinese word order: Subject + Time + Verb + Object.

G1.　美国饭，球，音乐，电影

G2.　明天晚上，这个週末，星期四，今天

G3.　去看，去听，去打，去吃

G4.　我们，我爸爸妈妈，小白和小高，王朋和李友

1. 小白和小高 今天 去吃 美国饭　　　　　　　。

2. 我们 星期四 去打 球　　　　　　　　　　　。

3. 我爸爸妈妈 明天晚上 去看 电影　　　　　　。

4. 王朋和李友 这个週末 去听 音乐.　　　　　　。

B. Please use "（没）有意思" to complete the following dialogues.

1. A: 你觉得昨天的电影 有意思　　　　　　　　　吗？

   B: 不，我觉得 昨天的电影 没有意思　　　　　。

2. A: 你想去看中国电影吗？

   B: 不想。我 想去看中国电影 没有意思　　　　。

3. A: 你为什么不听中国音乐？
   　　　　　　　　　　yīn yuè

   B: 因为 我觉得中国音乐 没有意思　　　　　　。

4. A: 今天晚上的电视都很 没有意思　，我们去唱歌，好不好？

   B: 我不想去，我 唱歌 没有意思　　　　　　　。

C. Please use " 因为...所以 " to answer the following questions.

1. *A:* 小高为什么请小白看电影？

   B: 因为是小白的生日,所以小高请小白看电影 。

2. *A:* 小张为什么不想去打球？

   B: 因为小张只喜欢乒乓,所以他不想去打球 。

3. *A:* 小张为什么不想去看电影？

   B: 因为小张很忙,所以他不去看电影 。

D. Please complete the following exchanges.

1. *A:* 你周末常常做什么？

   B: 我周末常常打球。

2. *A:* 你喜欢看美国电影还是外国电影？

   B: 我两都喜欢看电影.

3. *A:* 星期一晚上的电影有意思还是星期六晚上的电影有意思？

   B: 星期六晚上的电影有意思。

4. *A:* 你今天晚上几点钟睡觉？

   B: 我今天晚上十二点钟睡觉。

5. *A:* 你觉得看书有意思还是看电视有意思？

   B: _____

E. Translate the following sentences into Chinese using the words and phrases given in the parentheses.

1. Do you like going dancing on weekends? (V+不+V)

   Nǐ zhōu mò xǐhuān bù xǐhuān tiào wǔ?

   你周末喜欢不喜欢跳舞？

2. I often invite my classmates to go to see foreign movies. (请...去 +V)

wài guó diàn yǐng.

我

3. I like singing and listening to music. Sometimes I also like reading.

我喜欢

4. Because it was your treat yesterday, I'll take you to dinner tomorrow.
   (因为...所以)

因为昨天你请,所以明天我请你吃饭.

5. Little Zhang, long time no see.

小张,好久不见 .

6. Do you feel like going to play ball this weekend? (V+不+V，去 +V)

xiang xiang

7. I don't like reading. I only like eating, watching TV and sleeping. (只)

8. I think this foreign movie is very interesting. (有意思)

9. Then forget it. I'll go to bed. (去)

开

10. I am busy today. I don't want to go to see the movie. (想)

我今天很忙。

11. I don't like foreign movies. I only like American movies. (只)

我不喜欢外国电影。我只喜欢美国电影。

12. Is tomorrow your younger brother's birthday (or not)? (V+不+V)

Ming tian shi bu shi ni didi de xengsheng ri ?

Section Two

A. List your hobbies in Chinese.

B. Describe in detail what you did last weekend.

C. Write a story which will include all five activities in the picture below.

Lesson Five   Visiting Friends

I. LISTENING COMPREHENSION

Section One (Listen to the tape for the textbook)

A. Dialogue (True/False)

(F) 1. Wang Peng had met Little Gao's older sister before.
(T) 2. Li You was very happy to meet Little Gao's younger sister.
(T) 3. Li You thought that Little Gao's house was nice and big.
(F) 4. Little Gao's older sister works in a restaurant.
(T) 5. Li You did not drink beer.
(F) 6. Little Gao's sister gave Li You a cola.
(F) 7. Li You did not drink anything at Little Gao's house.

B. Narrative (True/False)

(T) 1. Little Gao's older sister works in a library.
(T) 2. Wang Peng had two glasses of beer at Little Gao's house.
(T) 3. Li You did not drink beer at Little Gao's house.
(T) 4. Wang Peng and Li You chatted and watched T.V. with Little Gao's sister last night.
(F) 5. Wang Peng and Li You left Little Gao's house at noon time.

Section Two (Listen to the tape for the workbook)

A. Dialogue I (True/False)

(   ) 1. The man and the woman run into each other in a library.
(   ) 2. The man and the woman have never met each other before.
(   ) 3. The man is looking for his younger brother.

B. Narrative (True/False)

(   ) 1. The speaker thinks that Little Bai and Little Li are old friends.
(   ) 2. The three people are most likely in the speaker's place.
(   ) 3. Little Bai told Little Li that he works in the library.

C. Dialogue II (Multiple choice)

(   ) 1. The dialogue most likely occurs in _____.
    a. a car
    b. a house
    c. a library
    d. a concert hall

(   ) 2. Which of the following statements about the woman is true?
    a. She doesn't like TV in general but she likes what is on TV tonight.
    b. She doesn't like TV in general and she likes what is on TV tonight even less.
    c. She likes TV in general but she doesn't like what is on TV tonight.
    d. She likes TV in general and she particularly likes what is on TV tonight.

53

(   ) 3. What will they most likely do for the rest of the evening?
      a. Watch TV
      b. Listen to American music
      c. Read an American novel
      d. Listen to Chinese music

D. Dialogue III (Multiple choice)
(   ) 1. Which of the following is the correct order of the woman's preferences?
      a. Coffee, tea, beer
      b. Beer, coffee, tea
      c. Coffee, beer, tea
      d. Tea, coffee, beer

(   ) 2. Which beverage does the man not have?
      a. Tea
      b. Beer
      c. Cola
      d. Coffee

(   ) 3. Which beverage does the woman finally get?
      a. Tea
      b. Beer
      c. Cola
      d. Coffee

E. Dialogue IV (Multiple choice)
(   ) 1. Where did they spend last Saturday evening? They were _____.
      a. at Little Bai's place
      b. at Little Gao's place
      c. at Little Li's place
      d. at Little Bai's brother's place

(   ) 2. What did Little Bai's brother do at the party? He was _____.
      a. drinking
      b. watching TV
      c. chatting
      d. dancing

(   ) 3. Little Bai spent most of the evening _____.
      a. drinking and watching TV
      b. chatting and watching TV
      c. drinking and chatting
      d. drinking, chatting and watching TV

II. SPEAKING EXERCISES

Section One (Answer the questions in Chinese based on the dialogues)

A. Dialogue

      1. Who went to Little Gao's house?

      2. Did Wang Peng and Li You know Little Gao's older sister before?

      3. What is Little Gao's older sister's name?

      4. How is Little Gao's house?

      5. Where does Little Gao's older sister work?

      6. What did Wang Peng want to drink?

      7. Why did Li You ask for a glass of water?

B. Narrative

      1. Why did Wang Peng and Li You go to Little Gao's house?

      2. Is Little Gao's older sister a teacher? Please explain.

      3. What did Wang Peng drink? How much?

      4. What did Wang Peng and Li You do at Little Gao's house?

      5. When did Wang Peng and Li You go home?

Section Two

A. This picture depicts a scene from Dialogue I of this lesson. Please act it out with some of your classmates.

B. You are talking with a classmate's brother/sister for the first time. Find out if he/she is a student, where he/she works, and what his/her hobbies are.

C. You are visiting a friend's room. Compliment the room. Your friend offers you something to drink, but you just want a glass of water.

D. Explain in Chinese that you went to a friend's house last night. Your friend works at the school library. You chatted and watched T.V. together and did not return home until 11:30 p.m.

III. Reading Comprehension

Section One

A. Please read the following description carefully and match each of the names with the
   proper beverage.

> 　　小高、小张和王朋都是同学，小高今年十九岁，
> 小张今年二十岁，王朋今年二十一岁。小高不喜欢喝
> 茶，小张不喝可乐，王朋喜欢喝咖啡、啤酒，但是不
> 喜欢喝茶。

小高　　　　茶
小张　　　　啤酒
王朋　　　　可乐

B. Read the following note, and answer the questions in English.

> 小张：
> 　　明天晚上七点半学校有一个中国电影，我们一起
> 去看，好吗？请你晚上来找我。
>
> *zhǎo*
> *look for*
>   小高
>   七月五日下午四点半
> *date*

1. Who wrote the note?　小高

2. What time is the movie shown?　七点半

3. Where is the movie shown?　学校

4. What date is the movie shown?　七月六日

5. When was the note written?　七月五日下午四点半

Section Two

A. Read the passage and answer the questions. (Multiple choice)

> 昨天是小李的生日，小李请了小高、小张和王朋三个同学去她家吃饭。小李的家很大，也很漂亮。小李的爸爸是老师，他很有意思。他们七点钟吃晚饭。小李的妈妈是医生，昨天很忙，九点才回家吃晚饭。小李的哥哥和姐姐都不在家吃饭。王朋和小李的爸爸妈妈一起喝茶、聊天。小高、小张和小李一起喝可乐、看电视。小高、小张和王朋十一点才回家。

(a) 1. Where did Little Gao go last night?
   a. Little Li's home
   b. Little Zhang's home
   c. Wang Peng's home
   d. His own home

(d) 2. Who was late for dinner last night?
   a. Little Gao
   b. Little Zhang
   c. Little Li's father
   d. Little Li's mother

(b) 3. Which of the following statements is true?
   a. Little Li's mother is a teacher.
   b. Little Li's father is an interesting person.
   c. Little Li's brother and sister were home last night.
   c. Wang Peng talked with Little Li all evening.

B. Read the passage and answer the questions. (True/False)

> 今天早上小高去找他的同学小张，小张介绍他妹妹认识了小高，小张的妹妹也是他们学校的学生。小张的妹妹很漂亮，喜欢唱歌和看书。这个週末小高想请小张的妹妹去喝咖啡、看电影。

(T) 1. Little Gao met Little Zhang's sister before.
(T) 2. Little Zhang and his sister are attending the same school.
(F) 3. Little Gao's sister likes dancing.
(F) 4. Little Gao would like to invite Little Zhang and his sister to see a movie this weekend.

IV. WRITING & GRAMMAR EXERCISES

Section One

A. Please answer the following questions.

1. A: 你常常在家看书还是在图书馆看书？

   B: 你常常在家看书 _____ 。

2. A: 你爸爸妈妈在哪儿工作？

   B: 我 _____ 。

3. A: 你喜欢喝茶还是喜欢喝咖啡？

   B: _____ 。

4. A: 你爸爸喜欢喝美国啤酒还是喜欢喝外国啤酒？

   B: _____ 。

B. Answer the following questions based on your own situation.

1. 你喜欢去同学家玩吗？为什么？

2. 你喜欢喝茶、可乐、咖啡还是啤酒？为什么？

3. 你喜欢在哪儿看书？

4. 你和你的同学常常一起做什么？

5. 昨天晚上你去没去朋友家玩儿？

C. Please use each group of the following words to make an interrogative sentence, a
   positive sentence, and a negative sentence.

Example: 小高家 / 大

==> a. 小高家大不大？
　　 b. 小高家很大。
　　 c. 小高家不大。

1. 这个医生 / 好

a. 这个医生好不好 ?
b. 这个医生很好 。
c. 这个医生不好 。

2. 小白的妹妹 / 漂亮

a. 小白的妹妹漂亮不漂亮 ?
b. 小白的妹妹很漂亮 。
c. 小白的妹妹不漂亮 。

3. 张律师 / 高兴

a. 张律师高兴不高兴 ?
b. 张律师很高兴 。
c. 张律师不高兴 。

4. 那个电影 / 有意思

a. 那个电影有没有意思 ?
b. 那个电影很有意 。
c. _____ 。

D. Change the following sentences from the positive to the negative.

Example: A：我昨天晚上看电视了。

   ===> B：我昨天晚上没(有)看电视。

1. A：他今天上午打球了。

   B：他今天上午没打球   。

2. A：我下午去小高家了。

   B：我下午没去小高家   。

3. A：上星期五是小高的生日，王朋喝啤酒了。

   B：上星期五是小高的生日王朋没喝啤酒   。

4. A：星期六他去图书馆了。

   B：星其六他没去图书馆   。

E. Answer the following questions in both the positive and the negative forms.

Example: A：你昨天晚上跳舞了吗？

         B1：我昨天晚上跳舞了。

         B2：我昨天晚上没(有)跳舞。

1. A：小李昨天晚上喝茶了吗？

   B1：她昨天晚喝茶了   。

   B2：她昨天晚上没喝茶   。

2. A：你上午喝咖啡了吗？

   B1：我上午喝咖啡了   。

   B2：我上午没喝咖啡   。

3. A：小白上星期回家了吗？

   B1：小白上星其回家了   。

   B2：小白上星其没回家   。

4. A：星期天小高去朋友家玩了吗？

   B1：星其天小高去朋友家玩了   。

   B2：星其天小高没去朋友家玩   。

F. Translate the following sentences into Chinese using the words and phrases in the parentheses when given.

1. Let me introduce you. This is my classmate.

   我介绍一下你，这是我的同学。

2. Very pleased to meet you. (认识)

   认识你很高兴。

3. Little Gao's home is very big and also very beautiful. (Adj.)

   小高家很大也很漂亮。

4. *A:* Where do you work? (在，哪儿)

   B: I work at the school.

5. Would you like to have some coffee? (点儿)

6. Would you like to drink cola or beer? (还是)

7. We got acquainted with Little Gao's older sister at the library. (在)

8. Last night they got together to drink and talk. (聊天)

   昨天晚上

9. Last night Little Zhang drank six bottles of beer. (了, measure word)

10. Little Bai does not like beer. He only drank two glasses of cola.

11. *A:* Why did you get home as late as twelve? （才）

为丨

B: Because I went to see a foreign movie.

12. Last night Wang Peng went to Li You's home for a visit. He met Li You's older sister.

13. Let's go home! （吧）

我们回家吧！

14. Let's eat dinner! （吧）

我们吃晚饭吧！

Section Two
A. List what you drink in Chinese.

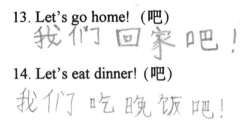

可口可乐   茶   水
kěkǒukělè   chá   shuǐ

B. Describe a recent visit to your friend's house. Make sure that you mention what you did and what you drank.

C. Translate the folllowing note into Chinese.
  "Yesterday evening I went to the library to read. In the library I met a girl. She is very pretty. We read together, and I didn't go home until eleven o'clock.

昨天晚上我

Lesson Six   Making Appointments

I. LISTENING COMPREHENSION

Section One (Listen to the tape for the textbook)

A. Dialogue I (Multiple choice)

(b) 1. Why does Li You call Teacher Wang?
   - a. Li You cannot come to school, because she is sick.
   - b. Li You wants to ask questions.
   - c. Li You wants to know where Teacher Wang's office is.
   - d. Li You wants to know where the meeting is.

(c) 2. What is Teacher Wang going to do this afternoon? He is going to_____.
   - a. teach two classes
   - b. go home early
   - c. attend a meeting
   - d. go to a doctor's office

(2) 3. How many classes will Teacher Wang teach tomorrow morning?
   - a. 1   b. 2   c. 3   d. 4

(b) 4. What will Teacher Wang be doing at 3:30 tomorrow afternoon?
   - a. Attending a meeting
   - b. Giving an exam
   - c. Working in his office
   - d. Seeing a doctor

(a) 5. Where is Li You going to meet Teacher Wang?
   - a. In Teacher Wang's office
   - b. In the classroom
   - c. In the meeting room
   - d. In the library

(d) 6. When will Li You meet with Teacher Wang tomorrow?
   - a. 9:00 a.m.
   - b. 10:30 a.m.
   - c. 3:00 p.m.
   - d. 4:30 p.m.

B. Dialogue II (True/False)

(T) 1. Li You is returning Wang Peng's phone call.
(F) 2. Wang Peng has an examination next week.
(T) 3. Li You is asking Wang Peng to practice Chinese with her.
(T) 4. Wang Peng is inviting Li You to have a coffee.
(F) 5. Wang Peng is going to have dinner with Li You this evening.
(T) 6. Wang Peng does not know exactly when he is going to call Li You.

63

我下个星期要考较

C. Listen to Dialogue II very carefuly to see if you can locate the phrase which the curved arrow on the upper left corner is trying to represent.

Section Two (Listen to the tape for the workbook)

A. Dialogue I (True/False)

(T) 1. Tomorrow will be Friday.

(F) 2. Li You cannot go for the dinner tomorrow because she will be busy.

(T) 3. Li You will be practicing Chinese this evening.

(F) 4. Wang Peng promises to help Li You with her Chinese tomorrow at 6 p.m.

B. Dialogue II (True/False)

(F) 1. The woman in the dialogue is the man's sister.

(T) 2. The telephone call was originally not meant for the woman.

(T) 3. There is going to be a Chinese film tonight.

(F) 4. The woman will most likely stay home tonight.

C. Dialogue III (Multiple choice)

(b) 1. Which of the following statements is true?

    a. The woman invites the man to join a dinner party at her home.

    b. The woman invites the man to attend a dance at her home.

    c. The woman hopes to join the dinner party at the man's home.

    d. The woman hopes to attend a dance at the man's home.

(b) 2. Why couldn't the man go?

    a. He is giving a party.

    b. He has a test.

    c. He has another dinner party to attend.

    d. He has another dance to attend.

D. Dialogue IV (True/False)

(T) 1. Wang Peng cannot help Li You practice Chinese because he will have class tomorrow afternoon.

(T) 2. Wang Peng asks Miss Bai to help Li You with her Chinese.

(F) 3. Miss Bai and Li You will meet at 2 p.m. tomorrow in the library.

II. SPEAKING EXERCISES

Section One (Answer the following questions in Chinese based on the text)

A. Dialogue I
1. Why did Li You call Teacher Wang?
2. Will Teacher Wang be free this afternoon? Please explain.
3. Will Teacher Wang be free tomorrow morning? Please explain.
4. What will Teacher Wang do at 3 o'clock tomorrow afternoon?
5. When will Li You go to visit Teacher Wang?
6. Where will Teacher Wang and Li You meet?

B. Dialogue II
1. Why did Li You call Wang Peng? Please explain.
2. Why did Wang Peng ask Li You to buy him some coffee?
3. What will Wang Peng do tonight?
4. When will Wang Peng call Li You?
5. Will Li You go to see a movie tonight? Please explain.

Section Two

A. You are calling your teacher and would like to make an appointment with him/her. Your teacher happens to be busy at the time you suggest. Ask your teacher when he/she will be available. Decide the time and place to meet.

B. You are calling a friend to ask for a favor and you promise to treat him/her to something in return. You would like to meet him/her tonight, but he/she is going to see a movie and does not know when he/she will be back. He/she promises that he/she will give you a call when he/she comes back.

C. You are calling a friend to ask a favor. Your friend is willing to help you. Decide the time and place to meet, and promise that you will take your friend out for a foreign movie.

D. Make an oral presentation in class describing this picture in detail. Feel free to borrow any sentences in the textbook. However, you are not allowed to look at the textbook when you make your presentation.

III. READING COMPREHENSION

Section One

A. Match the replies on the left with the appropriate expressions on the right. Write down the letter in the parentheses.

(E) 1. 认识你们我也很高兴。
(F) 2. 不客气。
(G) 3. 再见。
(C) 4. 对不起,我不喝酒。
(D) 5. 对不起,小白不在。
(H) 6. 对不起,我今天下午要开会。
(B) 7. 对不起,我明天要考试。
(A) 8. 我是王朋。

A. 你是哪位?
B. 我们今天晚上去跳舞,好吗?
C. 喝点儿酒,怎么样?
D. 喂,请问小白在吗?
E. 认识你很高兴。
F. 谢谢。
G. 明天见。
H. 今天下午我来找你,好吗?

B. Read the passage and answer the questions. (True/False)

李友是张老师的学生。今天上午李友给张老师打电话,因为她下个星期考试,想问张老师几个问题。可是张老师今天下午有课,没有时间见李友。张老师明天上午要开会,下午有两节课,三点半以後才有空。张老师说李友可以四点以後到办公室去找他。

(F) 1. 今天上午 张老师给李友打电话。
(T) 2. 张老师下个星期要给学生考试。
(F) 3. 张老师今天下午要开会。
(F) 4. 张老师明天三点没空。
(T) 5. 张老师明天下午四点以后在办公室。

C. Read the passage and answer the questions (True/False)

小张今天很忙,上午有四节课,中午跟同学一起吃饭,下午在图书馆看书,跟小李练习中文,晚上到小白的学校看电影,十一点才回家。因为明天他有两个考试,所以今天晚上他没有时间睡觉。

( ) 1. 小张上午有空。
( ) 2. 小张下午不在家。
( ) 3. 小张晚上跟小李一起练习中文。
( ) 4. 小张晚上到小白学校的图书馆看书。
( ) 5. 小张今天晚上不睡觉,因为他明天要考试。

Section Two

A. Read the following note and answer the questions. (True/False)

这是小王今天要做的事：

8:00 中文课 *Chinese class*

10:00 去白老师办公室 *go to teacher's office*

14:30 看王医生 *see Dr. Wang*

16:00 开会 *Have meeting*

18:00 跟小李吃饭

20:30 请小李喝咖啡 *Invite Li for coffee*

23:15 跟小张去学校看电影

(T) 1. 小王今天只有一节课。

(   ) 2. 小王要跟小李一起吃午饭。

(   ) 3. 小王上午要找白老师。

(   ) 4. 今天晚上小李要请小王喝咖啡。

(   ) 5. 今天晚上小王要晚上十二点以後才回家。

B. Read this note, and answer the following questions. (Multiple choice)

小高：

　　小张下午打电话给你了。他想请你星期四下午帮他练习中文，不知道你有没有空。回来以后给他打电话，他的电话是324-6597。

姐姐

三月八号（星期二）下午三点

(c) 1. Who wrote the note?
       a. 小高。
       b. 小张。
       c. 小高的姐姐。
       d. 小张的姐姐。

(   ) 2. Which of the following is true?
       a. 小张星期四下午给小高打了电话。
       b. 小高知道星期四下午要帮 小张练习说中文。
       c. 小高的姐姐请小高回来以后 给小张打电话。
       d. 小高的姐姐给小张打了电话。

(   ) 3. Which of the following is true?
       a. 明天是星期四。
       b. 明天是三月九号。
       c. 三月八号是星期四。
       d. 三月十号是星期二。

C. Authentic Materials:

Below is a page of Little Gao's appointment book. Take a look at the things that he plans to do this week and answer the following questions in English.

1. 他星期天在哪儿吃饭？

Going to dinner on Saturday.

2. 他什么时候考中文？

He has class on Tuesday.

3. 他跟王朋在哪儿练习中文？

4. 他姐姐的生日是几月几号？

5. 他星期五下午有什么事？

6. 他请谁喝咖啡？

7. 他们星期几喝咖啡？

8. 他们什么时候喝咖啡？

9. 他星期天要去哪儿？

D. Take another look at Little Gao's appoinment book. Do you know what he is supposed to do on Monday morning? There is only character which we haven't learned yet. Please circle that character. That character was used as the phonetic elementary in another character in L. 4. What does the character mean in that sentence? Can you guess it's pronunciation?

IV. WRITING & GRAMMAR EXERCISES

Section One

A. Please fill in the blanks with appropriate measure words.

两（个）问题

您是哪（位）？

三（节）课

四（杯）茶 (cup)

五（瓶）啤酒 (bottle)

B. Following the example, make sentences using the given words and 得.

　　Example:为什么今天晚上你不去跳舞？（看书）

　　===>因为今天晚上我得看书。

1.为什么你不睡觉？（等我妹妹的电话）

因为我得等我妹妹的电话。

2.为什么你不喝啤酒？（下午上课）

因为下午我得上课.

3.为什么你今天下午没有空儿？（开会）

因为今天下午我得开会.

C. Please answer the following questions.

1.谁常常给你打电话?

我姐姐常常给我打电话.

2.你是大学几年级的学生？

3.你星期四几点钟有中文课？

一点钟我有中文课.

4.你星期一有几节课？

我星期一有两节课.

5. 你明天有没有考试？

我明天我没有考试。

6. 你知道不知道你的中文老师叫什么名字？

to know

她叫 Michelle Tang.

7. 你喜欢跟同学一起去跳舞吗？

D. Please use 要是 to answer the following questions.

1. 要是你明天没课，你想做什么？

要是我明天没课，我想到家去。

2. 要是今天你们的老师请你们吃饭，你想吃美国饭还是吃中国饭？

要是今天我们的老师请我们吃饭，我想吃中国饭。

3. 要是你明天考试，你想在图书馆还是在家看书？

4. 要是别人说谢谢你，你说什么？

要是别人说谢谢我，我说不客气。

5. 要是你有空，你想去看电影还是想去打球？

E. Please use 但是 to complete the following questions.

1. 我想今天下午去找王老师，_____。

2. 我想这个周末去看电影，_____。

3. 我想请我的同学帮忙，_____。

4. 我想给你打电话，_____。

F. Rearrange the following Chinese words into sentences, using the given English sentences as clues.

1. 四点 / 我 / 办公室 / 电话 / 在 / 明天 / 等 / 以後 / 下午 / 你的
   (I will be waiting for your phone call in the office after 4:00 p.m. tomorrow.)

   明天下午以後四点我在办公室等你的电话。

2. 有人 / 不知道 / 请我 / 晚上 / 回来 / 什么 / 时候 / 今天 / 吃晚饭
   (Someone is taking me out for dinner this evening. I don't know when I will be back.)

3. 您 / 回来 / 给我 / 方便 / 请 / 以后 / 打 / 要是 / 电话
   (If it is convenient for you, please give me a call after you come back.)

G. Translate the following sentences into Chinese using the given words and phrases in the parentheses.

1. This morning my teacher called me. (给，了)

   这个上午我的老师给我打了。

2. Teacher, are you free this weekend? I'd like to invite you to a dinner.
   (有时间，请)

   老师,这个周末您有时间吗?我请您吃饭.

3. Don't go to his office. (别)

   你别到他的办公室去!

4. When will you be free this weekend? (有空儿)

   这个周末你什么时候有空儿?

5. This afternoon I went to look for Teacher Zhang, but he wasn't in his office.
   (可是，在)

   找

   今天下午

6. Tomorrow afternoon I have two classes. I won't be free until after three thirty.
   （以后，才）

7. This afternoon I have to give an exam to the first-year class. （要）

8. If it's convenient for you, I will go to your office to wait for you at 4:00 p.m.
   Is that all right? （要是，去）

9. Because I need to take a Chinese exam next Thursday, I'd like to ask Wang
   Peng to help me practice speaking Chinese this weekend.
   （因为...所以，请，帮）

10. I'll wait for you, but you have to treat me to the movie. （但是，得）

11. I'll go look for you after I get back. （以后）

12. I'll wait for your call after I get back home. （以后，等）

13. Buy you a dinner? No problem!
   我请你吃饭，没问题！

14. Sorry! I will not be free next week.
   对不起，

Section Two

A. List the things that you need to do today. Don't forget to give the time.

B. Write a note to your Chinese friend to see if he/she can practice Chinese with you tomorrow evening. Promise him/her that you will buy him/her coffee afterwards.

C. Write a description of Little Wang's life. Little Wang is often busy. He likes to see movies, but he has no time; he also likes to listen to music, but no time, either. Tomorrow he will be free. He will take Miss Bai out for dinner tomorrow evening. He doesn't know when she will be back home tomorrow afternoon, but he will wait for her call.

Lesson Seven   Studying Chinese

I. LISTENING COMPREHENSION

Section One (Listen to the tape for the textbook) (True/False)

A. Dialogue I
(　) 1. Li You didn't do very well on her test last week.
(　) 2. Wang Peng writes Chinese well, but very slowly.
(　) 3. Wang Peng didn't want to teach Li You how to write Chinese characters.
(　) 4. Li You has prepared for tomorrow's lesson.
(　) 5. The Chinese characters of Lesson Seven are very easy.
(　) 6. Li You has no problems with Lesson Seven's grammar.

B. Dialogue II
(　) 1. Little Bai is always late.
(　) 2. Little Bai didn't go to bed until after midnight last night.
(　) 3. Li You went to bed very late, because she was studying Chinese.
(　) 4. Little Bai has a very good Chinese friend.
(　) 5. Li You recited the lesson well, because she listened to the recording the night before.
(　) 6. Li You has a very handsome Chinese friend.

Section Two (Listen to the tape for the Workbook) (True/False)

A. Narrative
(　) 1. Mr. Li is an American
(　) 2. Mr. Li likes studying Chinese, but not English.
(　) 3. Mr. Li feels that English grammar is not too difficult, but Chinese grammar is hard.
(　) 4. Mr. Li is having a hard time learning Chinese characters.

B. Dialogue I (Little Wang is talking to Little Bai.)
(　) 1. Little Bai didn't do very well on the Chinese test last week.
(　) 2. Little Wang is not willing to practice Chinese with Little Bai.
(　) 3. Little Bai is very good at Chinese characters.
(　) 4. Little Wang can help Little Bai with both speaking and writing.

C. Dialogue II (Little Li is talking to Little Zhang.)
(　) 1. Little Zhang usually comes early.
(　) 2. Little Zhang previewed Lesson Eight.
(　) 3. Little Zhang went to bed early because he didn't have homework last night.
(　) 4. Little Zhang usually goes to bed before midnight.

II. SPEAKING EXERCISES

Section One (Answer the questions in Chinese based on the dialogues)

A. Dialogue I
1. How did Li You do on last week's test, and why?
2. Why did Wang Peng offer to help Li You with her writing of Chinese characters?
3. Who can write Chinese characters fast?
4. Which lesson will Li You study tomorrow?
5. How did Li You feel about the grammar, vocabulary and characters when she prepared the lesson?
6. What did Wang Peng and Li You do tonight?

B. Dialogue II
1. Why did Little Bai come so late today?
2. Why was Li You able to go to bed early last night?
3. Why did Little Bai say that it is nice to have a Chinese friend?
4. Which lesson the class is studying today?
5. Who did not listen to the recording last night?
6. How did Little Bai describe Li You's friend?

Section Two

A. Discuss the results of the recent Chinese tests with your friend. Comment on how you did on grammar, vocabulary and Chinese characters.

B. Find out why your friend is late or early for the class, and how he/she prepares for the new lesson.

C. Make up a story based on the two pictures below. Try to use the new words and sentence structures that you have learned in this lesson.

III. READING COMPREHENSION

Section One

A. Read Li You's schedule for Monday and answer the questions. (True/False)

早上	八点半	预习生词
	九点	听录音
	十点	上中文课
中午	十二点	吃午饭
下午	一点	睡午觉
	两点	复习中文
晚上	六点	吃晚饭
	八点	做功课

(F) 1. 李友星期一没有课。

( ) 2. 李友星期一上午预习生词。

( ) 3. 李友星期一下午听录音。

( ) 4. 李友一点钟吃午饭。

( ) 5. 李友吃晚饭以后做功课。

( ) 6. 李友复习中文以后睡午觉。

B. Read the passage and answer the questions. (True/False)

> 小王：
>
> 　　你好！我上个星期有个中文考试，我考得不太好，老师说我汉字写得不错，可是太慢。中文语法也有一点儿难，我不太懂。这个周末你有时间吗？我想请你帮助我复习中文。我们一起练习说中文，好吗？
>
> 　　　　　　　　　　　　小白
>
> 　　　　　　　　　　　　十月二十七日

(   ) 1. 小白上个星期考试考得不错。

(   ) 2. 老师说小白写汉字写得很好，也很快。

(   ) 3. 小白觉得中文语法很容易，她都懂。

(   ) 4. 小白要小王帮助她复习中文。

Section Two

A. Read the passage and answer the questions. (True/False)

> 昨天是小高的生日，李友和王朋都到小高家去了。他们一起喝啤酒，听音乐，唱歌，晚上十二点才回家，一点钟才睡觉。因为李友没有复习中文，所以今天考试考得不好。

(   ) 1. 昨天晚上小高十二点才回家。

(   ) 2. 昨天晚上十点钟王朋和李友都不在家。

(   ) 3. 今天李友有个中文考试。

(   ) 4. 王朋和李友昨天晚上睡觉睡得很早。

B. Read the passage and answer the questions. (True/False)

> 今天上午，小李预习了第六课。第六课的语法有点儿难，生词也很多。下午她要去老师的办公室问问题。她觉得学中文很有意思。说中国话不太难，可是汉字有一点儿难。

(   ) 1. 第六课的生词很多，语法也不容易。

(   ) 2. 今天下午他要去见老师。

(   ) 3. 小李觉得中文不难，可是没有意思。

(   ) 4. 小李觉得汉字不太容易。

IV. WRITING AND GRAMMAR EXERCISES

Section One

A. Answer the following questions.

> Example: *A:* 你昨天睡觉睡得晚吗？
>
> *B:* 我睡得很晚。

1. *A:* 你写字写得快吗？

   B: _____ 。

2. *A:* 你妹妹唱歌唱得好吗？

   B: _____ 。

3. *A:* 你哥哥打球打得好吗？

   B: _____ 。

4. *A:* 她跳舞跳得怎么样？

   B: _____ 。

5. *A:* 你说中文说得怎么样？

   B: _____ 。

6. *A:* 你的老师念课文念得怎么样？

   B: _____ 。

B. Fill in the blanks.

我和我的姐姐 _____ (both) 喜欢听 _____ (music)。我们 _____ (often) _____ (together) 听。我们 _____ (also) 喜欢 _____ (study) 中文。_____ (however)， 中国人说中文说得 _____ (too) 快。我 _____ (feel) 语法也 _____ (a bit) 难。

C. Complete the sentences with 才 or 就:

Example: 我们三点开会，可是<u>李小姐四点才来</u>。（才）
            我们三点开会，可是<u>李小姐两点就来了</u>。（就）

1. 我们八点钟有中文课，可是＿＿＿＿＿＿＿＿＿＿＿＿＿＿。（才）

2. 小王今天下午没有课，所以＿＿＿＿＿＿＿＿＿＿＿＿＿。（就）

3. 我昨天晚上去朋友家玩儿，＿＿＿＿＿＿＿＿＿＿＿＿＿。（才）

4. 她妈妈说明天来，可是＿＿＿＿＿＿＿＿＿＿＿＿＿＿＿。（就）

5. 因为我今天有考试，所以我昨天＿＿＿＿＿＿＿＿＿＿＿。（才）

6. 我哥哥说今天晚上给我打电话，可是＿＿＿＿＿＿＿＿＿＿＿＿＿＿＿＿＿＿＿＿＿＿＿＿＿＿＿＿。（就）

D. Complete the sentences with 因为 or 所以.

1. 因为昨天晚上没有功课，＿＿＿＿＿＿＿＿＿＿＿＿＿＿＿。

2. 因为你有中国朋友帮助你复习，＿＿＿＿＿＿＿＿＿＿＿＿。

3. A: 你怎么没去看电影？

   B: ＿＿＿＿＿＿＿＿＿＿＿＿＿＿＿＿。

4. A: 你为什麼请他喝咖啡？

   B: ＿＿＿＿＿＿＿＿＿＿＿＿＿＿＿＿。

5. ＿＿＿＿＿＿＿＿＿＿＿＿＿＿＿＿＿＿，所以他很晚才睡觉。

E. Fill in the blanks with 真 or 太.

1. 你这张照片_____漂亮。

2. 那个学校_____大了。

3. 今天的功课_____多了。

4. 这个工作_____有意思。

5. 第六课的生词_____多。

6. 李友的妈妈_____客气了。

F. Make sentences using the given words and 得.

　　Example: 说中文/好 ===>他说中文说得很好。

1. 写字/好

2. 说英文/快

3. 打球/不好

4. 学汉字/不太快

5. 喝啤酒/多

G. Translate the following sentences into Chinese.

1. The teacher writes Chinese characters very well.

2. Last night I was not back home until 10 o'clock. (就/才)

3. How come your younger brother didn't go to the movie on Wednesday?

4. She feels that Chinese grammar is a little bit hard. (有一点儿)

5. Because I am very busy, I will not go to the library until tomorrow afternoon. (就/才)

6. I went to the school (as early as) at seven o'clock today.

7. His older sister sings really well. (真)

8. You write the characters too slowly. (太...了)

9. I feel that the text of Lesson Six is a little difficult.

10. *A:* How come you are so happy today? (怎么)

   B: Because I did very well on the test. (得)

Section Two

A. Write a paragraph (5-10 sentences) describing your experience of learning Chinese.

B. List your daily activities starting from the time you get up and ending with the time you go to bed.

C. Write a paragraph in Chinese explaining the following: My younger sister did not learn Chinese well. She didn't like listening to the recording, so her pronunciation was not good. She didn't like studying grammar or writing the characters. That was why she didn't do well on the examination. But after she met a Chinese friend, they often practice speaking Chinese in the library. Now, she likes listening to the tape and writing the characters.

Lesson Eight   School Life

I. LISTENING COMPREHENSION

Section One (Listen to the tape for the textbook)

A. The Diary (Multiple choice)

(   ) 1. Which day of the week is August 10th?
       a. Monday   b. Tuesday   c. Wednesday   d. Thursday

(   ) 2. What did Li You do this morning before breakfast?
       a. She took a bath.
       b. She listened to the recording.
       c. She read the newspaper.
       d. She talked to her friend on the phone.

(   ) 3. What time did Li You go to the class this morning?
       a. 7:30   b. 8:00   c. 8:30   d. 9:00

(   ) 4. What did Li You NOT do in her Chinese class?
       a. Take a vocabulary test.
       b. Practice pronunciation.
       c. Learn characters.
       d. Study grammar.

(   ) 5. What class did Li You think was difficult?
       a. Chinese   b. Computer science
       c. American history   d. Economics

(   ) 6. Where did Li You have lunch today?
       a. At a Chinese restaurant.
       b. In the school's dining hall.
       c. At home.
       d. At her friend's house.

(   ) 7. What was Li You doing around 4:30 p.m.?
       a. Practicing Chinese.
       b. Reading a newspaper.
       c. Playing ball.
       d. Drinking coffee.

(   ) 8. What time did Li You eat her dinner?
       a. 5:45   b. 6:00   c. 6:30   d. 7:30

(   ) 9. What time did Li You return home tonight?
       a. 7:30   b. 8:30   c. 9:30   d. 10:30

85

(   ) 10. What did Li You do before she went to bed?
        a. Visited Little Lin.
        b. Did her homework.
        c. Talked to Wang Peng on the phone.
        d. Prepared for her test.

B. The letter (True/False).
(   ) 1. This is a letter from Yiwen to Miss Zhang.
(   ) 2. Yiwen's major is Chinese.
(   ) 3. Yiwen does not like her Chinese class at all.
(   ) 4. Yiwen's Chinese friend speaks very clearly.
(   ) 5. Yiwen is learning Chinese fast, because she has a Chinese friend.
(   ) 6. Yiwen would like Miss Zhang to attend her school concert.

C. Use numbers 1-3 to put the pictures in the correct sequence based on the information given in Dialogue II.

     (   )   (   )   (   )

Section Two (Listen to the tape for the workbook) (True/False)

A. Dialogue

(   ) 1. Li You is going to Teacher Zhang's office at 4:00 p.m. today.
(   ) 2. Wang Peng will be attending a class at 2:30 p.m. today.
(   ) 3. Li You plans to read newspapers in the library this evening.
(   ) 4. Li You and Wang Peng will see each other in the library this evening.

B. Narrative

(   ) 1. Wang Peng went to the library to help Li You with her Chinese.
(   ) 2. Wang Peng did not go to play ball this afternoon until he had finished his homework.
(   ) 3. Li You went to a movie with Wang Peng this evening.
(   ) 4. Li You has a Chinese class tomorrow.

II. SPEAKING EXERCISES

Section One (Answer the questions in Chinese based on the texts)

A. *The Diary*
1. When was the diary written?
2. What time did Li You get up on that day?
3. What did Li You do before 9:00 a.m. on that day?
4. What did Li You do in her Chinese class on that day?
5. Did Li You like her computer class? Why?
6. What did Li You do during the lunch hour?
7. What did Li You do that afternoon?
8. Please describe what Li You did that evening.

B. *The Letter*
1. Why is Yiwen so busy this semester?
2. Please describe Yiwen's Chinese class.
3. Is Yiwen making progress in her Chinese class? Why?
4. Why did Yiwen ask Miss Zhang if she likes music?
5. Do you think Yiwen has confidence in her Chinese? Why?

Section Two

A. Call your Chinese friend, and describe to him/her what you did yesterday at school.

B. Describe your Chinese class to your friend in great detail. Make sure to comment on how you feel about pronunciation, grammar, vocabulary, and Chinese characters.

C. Tell a atory based on the pictures below. Don't forget to mention the times.

III. READING COMPREHENSION

Section One (Answer the questions about the texts in English.)

A. *The Diary*

    1. 这是几月几号的日记？

    2. 李友早上开始听录音以前做了什么事？

    3. 今天上午李友有几节课？是什么课？

    4. 李友中午在哪儿吃饭？

    5. 李友下午在图书馆做什么？

    6. 李友跟谁一起打球？

    7. 李友为什么去找小林？

    8. 李友告诉王朋什么事？

B. *The Letter*

1. 写信的人叫什么名字？

2. 你觉得意文喜欢她的中文课吗？为什么？

3. 上中文课的时候意文能说英文吗？

4. 意文常常跟谁一起练习说中文？

5. 意文为什么给张小姐写信？

Section Two
A. Read the following and answer the questions. (True/False)

小张今天要做的事：
8:00　　　复习第七课生词、语法
9:00　　　上电脑课
10:00　　去王老师办公室练习发音
14:30　　去图书馆看报
16:00　　去打球
18:00　　去宿舍餐厅吃饭
20:15　　给小李打电话，请他一起练习中文
21:30　　写信给爸爸妈妈

( ) 1. 小张今天只有一节课。

( ) 2. 小张跟小林一起吃午饭。

( ) 3. 小张上午去见王老师。

( ) 4. 小张去小李家练习中文。

( ) 5. 小张吃晚饭以前去看打球。

( ) 6. 小张去图书馆以後去找王老师。

( ) 7. 小张睡觉以前给爸爸妈妈写信。

( ) 8. 小张练习中文以後才吃饭。

B. Read the note and answer the questions. (True/False)

小王：

　　今天晚上七点半学校有一个很好的音乐会，我想请你跟我一起去。请你回来以後给我打电话。我的电话是：八五七九五六三。

小谢
七月五日下午四点半

( ) 1. 电影七点半开始。

( ) 2. 今天晚上小谢要看一个中国电影。

( ) 3. 小谢没有电话。

( ) 4. 小王下午四点半来找小谢。

C. Read the passage and answer the questions. (True/False)

小张今天很忙，上午三节课以外，还有一个电脑考试。中午跟朋友一起吃饭，下午在图书馆看书，做功课，晚上在电脑室工作，十点钟回家吃晚饭。晚饭以后，他一边看电视，一边预习明天的功课，十二点半睡觉。

( ) 1. 小张上午没空。

( ) 2. 小张下午不在家，在图书馆看报。

( ) 3. 小张晚上很晚才吃饭。

( ) 4. 小张晚上在电脑室预习明天的功课。

( ) 5. 小张一边听音乐，一边看书。

D. Read the passage and answer the questions. (True/False)

小林以前常常跟朋友一起打球，聊天，看电视，不做功课。可是因为他下星期要考试，所以这个星期他不打球，不看电视，也不找朋友聊天，一个人到图书馆去看书。他很早就起床，很晚才睡觉，所以他上课的时候常常想睡觉。

( ) 1. 小林以前常常不做功课。

( ) 2. 小林常常跟朋友到图书馆去看书。

( ) 3. 小林这个星期除了不打球不看电视以外，也不找朋友聊天儿。

( ) 4. 因为小林不喜欢上课，所以他上课的时候想睡觉。

( ) 5. 这个星期小林睡觉睡得很早。

IV. WRITING AND GRAMMAR EXERCISES

Section One

A. Complete the following dialogues, and each sentence should contain a structure of double objects.

Example: *A:* 他教<u>谁</u>中文？

B: 他教<u>他弟弟</u>中文。

1. *A:* 王老师教学生_____？

    B: 王老师教_____。

2. *A:* 小高给____一本书？

    B: 小高给_____。

3. *A:* 李友问谁_____？

    B: 李友问_____。

4. *A:* 高小音给____一杯茶？

    B: 高小音给_____。

5. *A:* 你告诉王朋_____了？

    B: 我告诉王朋_____。

B. Follow the model and rewrite the sentences.

Example: 他吃饭的时候听音乐。

===> 他一边吃饭一边听音乐。

1. 他听音乐的时候看报。

2. 我们吃饭的时候练习说中文。

3. 我的朋友喜欢写字的时候听音乐。

4. 张小姐吃饭的时候看电视。

C. Follow the model and combine the sentences in each group into one that contains the structure "除了...还."

Example: 我学中文。我也学日文。

===>除了中文以外，我还学日文。

1. 我喜欢听音乐。我也喜欢跳舞。

2. 他常常打球。他也常常看电影。

3. 今天晚上我想写信。今天晚上我也想给我妈妈打电话。

4. 明天我有一节电脑课。明天我也有两节英文课。

5. 他预习了生词。他也预习了课文。

6. 我喜欢打球。我也喜欢找朋友聊天。

D. Answer the questions.

1. 除了中文课以外，你还有什么课？

2. 你常常跟谁一起去看电影？

3. 你睡觉以前做什么？

4. 你起床以后做什么？

E. Translate the following sentences into Chinese.

   1. My older sister taught me to sing, and I taught her to dance. (double objects)

   2. The teacher gave us a lot of homework.

   3. I hope that you can go to the concert with me.

   4. We practice speaking Chinese while playing ball. (一边...一边...)

   5. In addition to pronunciation, Mr. Wang also teaches us grammar.
     (除了...也...)

   6. Wang Peng read the text very well. (complement with 得)

   7. She wrote her Chinese diary poorly. (complement with 得)

   8. When I went to see her, she was calling her boyfriend.
     (...的时候，...正在...)

9. *A:* I'd like to go to the dining hall to have lunch. How about you?
   (到... 去+V)

   B: I had lunch as early as eleven. (就) I want to go to the library to read the newspapers. (到... 去+V)

10. He listened to the recording while having breakfast. (一边... 一边...)

11. I take a bath before I go to bed. (就)

12. Li You dances very well, but she does not dance much.
    (complement with 得; 不常)

13. I go to class after breakfast. (以后)

14. When I went to Little Lin's dorm yesterday morning, she was chatting with Little Bai. (... 的时候，... 正在...)

Section Two

A. Write your friend a letter in Chinese telling him/her about your experience of learning Chinese. "My Chinese class is hard, but I think it is pretty interesting. My Chinese friend often helps me, and that is the reason my Chinese has improved rapidly. In addition to practicing speaking Chinese, I also play ball and go to movies with my friend. Both my friend and I are happy."

B. Write a piece of diary in Chinese about your school life.

Lesson Nine   Shopping

I. LISTENING COMPREHENSION

Section One (Listen to the tape for the textbook) (Multiple choice)

A. Dialogue I
(   ) 1. What color shirt does the customer want to buy?
      a. Black   b. White   c. Red   d. Yellow

(   ) 2. What else does the customer want to buy besides the shirt?
      a. A hat   b. a pair of shoes
      c. a sweater   d. a pair of pants

(   ) 3. What size does the customer wear?
      a. Small   b. Medium   c. Large   d. Extra large

(   ) 4. How much does the customer need to pay altogether?
      a. Between $20 and $30.
      b. Between $30 and $40.
      c. Between $40 and $50.
      d. Between $50 and $60.

B. Dialogue II
(   ) 1. Why did the lady want to exchange the shoes?
      a. The shoes do not fit well.
      b. The shoes are damaged.
      c. She does not like the price.
      d. She does not like the color.

(   ) 2. What color does the lady prefer?
      a. Black   b. White   c. Brown   d. Red

(   ) 3. In what way are the new pair of shoes like the old pair? They are of _____.
      a. the same size   b. the same color
      c. the same price   d. the same design

C. Listening to the two dialogue in this lesson and decide which dialogue the pictures on the next page are depicting. Sequencing the four pictures based on the dialogue by using numbers 1-4.

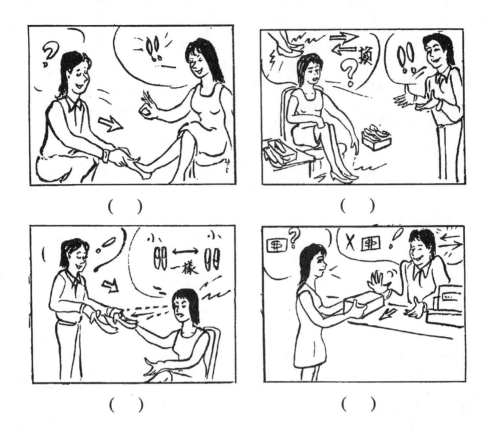

( )   ( )

( )   ( )

Section Two (Listen to the tape for the workbook)

A. Narrative (Multiple choice)

( ) 1. What color does Wang Peng Like?
   a. Blue   b. Brown   c. White   d. Red

( ) 2. Why does Wang Peng not like the shirt? Because of the _____.
   a. price   b. style   c. color   d. size

( ) 3. What colors are the shirts that the salesperson says they have?
   a. White, blue, and brown.
   b. White, red, and brown.
   c. Red, blue, and white.
   d. White, red, and yellow.

( ) 4. When did Wang Peng buy that shirt?
   a. 5 days ago   b. 7 days ago
   c. 10 days ago   d. 14 days ago

B. Dialogue (True/False)

( ) 1. The man returned his shirt for a different one, because he didn't like the color.
( ) 2. The man finally took a yellow shirt because he liked the color.
( ) 3. All the large-sized shirts in the store are yellow ones.
( ) 4. A large-sized shirt fits the man well.

II. SPEAKING EXERCISES

Section One (Answer the questions in Chinese based on the dialogues.)

A. Dialogue I
     1. What does the lady want to buy?
     2. Is the lady very rich? How do you know?
     3. Please give the price for each item, and the cost in total.
     4. If the lady gives the salesperson $100, how much change should she receive?

B. Dialogue II
     1. Why did the lady want to return the shoes for a different pair?
     2. Does the lady like black shoes? Please explain.
     3. What color shoes did she finally accept? Why?
     4. Did the lady pay any additional money for the new shoes? Please explain.

Section Two
A. Describe the clothes you are wearing today.

B. You are in a department store, trying to buy a shirt and a pair of pants. Tell the salesperson what color and size you want.

C. You bought a shirt that is too big. Try to exchange for a smaller one.

D. Describe the four pictures below without looking at the textbook.

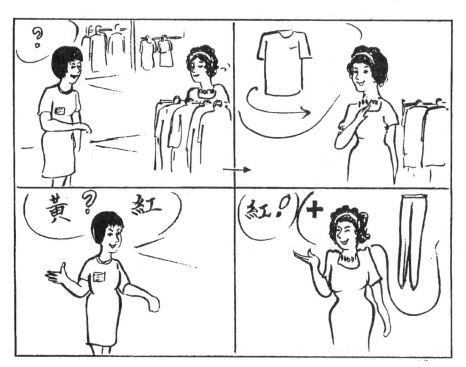

III. READING COMPREHENSION

Section One (Answer the questions about the dialogues.)

A. Dialogue I

1. 李小姐想买什么东西？

2. 她买了什么颜色的衬衫？

3. 她买了多大的裤子？

4. 衬衫一件多少钱？裤子一条多少钱？

5. 售货员找了多少钱给李小姐？

B. Dialogue II

1. 李小姐为什么想换鞋？

2. 李小姐想换什么颜色的鞋？

3. 李小姐换了鞋没有？她换了一双什么鞋？

Section Two

A. Read the passage and answer the questions.

上星期六，小张买了一条裤子，她想买黑色的，可是只有黄的和红的。她买了一条红的，回家以后，觉得不太喜欢那条裤子的颜色，她想明天下午去换一条别的裤子。

1. 上星期六小张买了什么颜色的裤子？

2. 小张喜欢什么颜色的裤子？

3. 小张为什么不喜欢她的新裤子？

4. 明天下午小张要做什么？

B. Read the passage and answer the questions (True/False).

李太太很喜欢买东西，她最喜欢买便宜的衣服。虽然她的衣服很多，可是都不太合适。李先生跟他太太不一样，他不喜欢买东西，也不常买东西。李先生只买大小合适的衣服，所以，李先生的衣服虽然不多，可是都很合适。

( ) 1. 李太太不喜欢买贵的衣服。

( ) 2. 李太太有很多衣服。

( ) 3. 李太太的衣服都很合适。

( ) 4. 李先生有便宜的衣服，也有贵的衣服。

( ) 5. 李先生没有很多衣服。

( ) 6. 李先生的衣服都太大了。

C. Find the corresponding clothing items to the expressions below. Put the alphabets in the parentheses next to them.

　　1. 鞋（　　）2. 裤子（　　）3. 外套（　　）4. 帽子（　　）5. 袜子（　　）

　　6. 裙子（　　）7. T-恤衫（　　）

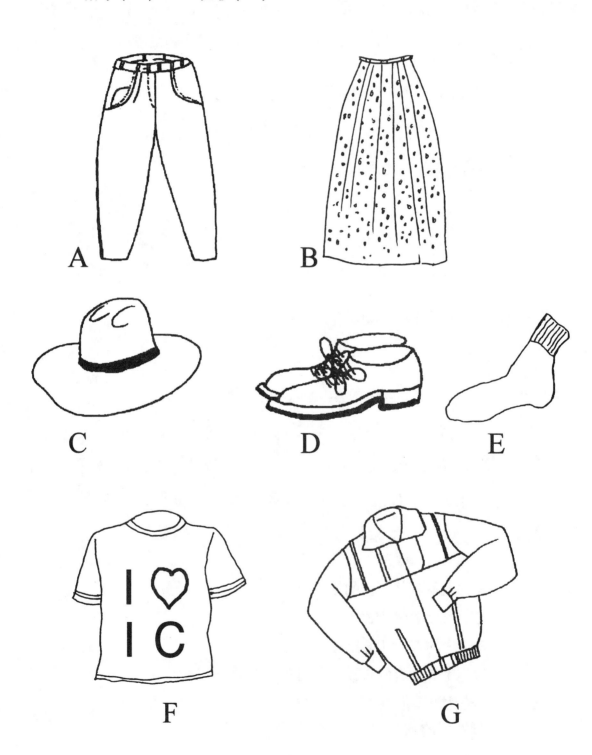

A

B

C

D

E

F

G

IV. WRITING AND GRAMMAR EXERCISES

Section One

A. Fill in each of the blanks with an appropriate measure word.

件，条，双，本，瓶，位，节，封，篇，杯

1. 一（　）鞋　　　　　　2. 一（　）衬衫

3. 两（　）裤子　　　　　4. 三（　）课

5. 一（　）先生　　　　　6. 一（　）书

7. 一（　）日记　　　　　8. 两（　）信

9. 一（　）可乐　　　　　10. 一（　）茶

B. Give Chinese characters for the following dollar amounts.

1. $5.12 _____

2. $18.50 _____

3. $70.05 _____

4. $99.99 _____

5. $100.60 _____

C. Complete the following sentences.

1. 这条裤子虽然颜色不太好 _____。(inexpensive)

2. 我虽然喜欢看电影，_____。(don't have time)

3. _____(very difficult)，可是我很喜欢学。

4. 虽然他上个月才开始学中文，_____。
   (speaks quite well)

5. _____ (I don't write well)，可是我很喜欢写汉字。

D. Follow the model and complete the following sentences using the pattern "A跟B一样 +Adj."

Example： 我的衬衫<u>跟我哥哥的衬衫一样贵</u>。（贵）

1. 这双鞋_____。（大）

2. 学英文_____。（有意思）

3. 我的裤子的颜色_____。（漂亮）

4. 你说中文_____。（快）

5. 第七课的功课_____。（难）

6. 学校餐厅的饭_____。（好吃）

E. Complete the following dialogue.

售货员：_____ ？
李小姐：我想买一条裤子。

售货员：_____ ？
李小姐：大号的。

售货员：这条太大了，你可以换_____。
李小姐：中号的很合适。

售货员：_____ ？
李小姐：还要买一双鞋。

售货员：_____ ？
李小姐：黄的。
售货员：一条裤子十九块，一双鞋十五块，一共_____。

李小姐：_____ 。
售货员：找您六十六块。

F. Translate the following sentences into Chinese.

1. Would you like to watch TV or listen to music? （想；还是）

2. That large-size shirt is my older brother's, and this small-size one is mine. (noun/pronoun ＋ 的)

3. The yellow shirts are expensive, and the white ones are cheap. (adj ＋ 的; adj as predicate)

4. I want a shirt, not too large, and not too small, either.

5. The new words in Lesson Nine are not too many, and not too few, either.

6. Do you want to buy a pair of black shoes or a pair of yellow ones? (还是)

7. A bottle of beer is $3.00 and a glass of cola is 75 cents. $3.75 altogether.

8. This pair of pants are as just expensive as that pair.

9. The color of your shirt is the same as mine.

10. Although this pair of shoes fit me well, I don't like the color. (虽然)

Section Two

A. Write a shopping list in Chinese, including the names and prices of the items you want to purchase.

B. Describe what you are wearing in Chinese. Don't forget to mention color and size.

C. Translate the following passage into Chinese.
   "Yesterday I bought a yellow shirt and a pair of blue pants. The pants are very very expensive, but the color is very nice and the size is right. Although the shirt is very pretty and also very cheap, but it's too small. Tomorrow I'll exchange for a bigger shirt."

Lesson Ten   Talking about the Weather

I. LISTENING COMPREHENSION

Section One (Listen to the tape for the textbook) (True/False)

A. Dialogue I
(   ) 1. It rained yesterday.
(   ) 2. The weather today is better than yesterday.
(   ) 3. It will be warmer tomorrow than today.
(   ) 4. Miss Li will go to see the red leaves tomorrow.
(   ) 5. Mr. Wang went to Shanghai by himself.
(   ) 6. The lady suggests that the man stay home tomorrow.

B. Dialogue II
(   ) 1. It has been raining often recently.
(   ) 2. The weather will be better next week.
(   ) 3. This weekend is not a good time to go out, for it is going to be cold and wet.
(   ) 4. It will be hotter in two months.
(   ) 5. Little Ye is in Taiwan for a visit.
(   ) 6. The best time to visit Taiwan is in spring.

Section Two (Listen to the tape for the workbook)

A. Dialogue I (Multiple choice)
(   ) 1. What season is it now?
    a. spring   b. summer   c. autumn   d. winter

(   ) 2. Where was the woman this afternoon?
    a. In the classroom   b. In the park
    c. In the shopping mall   d. In the office

(   ) 3. How will the weather be tomorrow? It will be _____.
    a. cold and rainy   b. hot and humid
    c. warm and sunny   d. rainy and windy

(   ) 4. The man got the information on the weather from _____.
    a. the T.V.   b. the newspaper
    c. his friend   d. the radio

B. Dialogue II (True/False)
(   ) 1. Wang Peng had an outing with Li You today.
(   ) 2. Wang Peng does not like the weather because it started to rain in the morning.
(   ) 3. The weather forecast says that the weather will be somewhat better tomorrow.
(   ) 4. Tomorrow Wang Peng will be preparing his lessons for Monday.
(   ) 5. Wang Peng believes that next Saturday it will be even cooler than tomorrow.
(   ) 6. The dialogue most likely occurred on a Sunday.

II. SPEAKING EXERCISES

Section One (Answer the questions in Chinese about the dialogues.)

A. Dialogue I
   1. What did the weather forecast say about the weather tomorrow?
   2. Was the man excited about tomorrow's weather forecast? Why?
   3. Where will Miss Li most likely be tomorrow?
   4. What did the woman suggest the man do tomorrow?

B. Dialogue II
   1. What did the newspaper say about the weather this week and next week?
   2. Why couldn't they go out to have fun this weekend?
   3. Please describe Taiwan's weather.
   4. Why is Little Xia not very familiar with the weather in Taiwan?

Section Two

A. Describe the climate of your hometown.

B. Compare the weather of your hometown with the weather of the place where you are now.

III. READING COMPREHENSION

Section One (Answer the questions about the dialogues.)

A. Dialogue I

1. 今天天气怎么样？

2. 高先生明天想做什么事？

3. 天气预报说明天的天气怎么样？

4. 高先生跟李小姐明天会去看红叶吗？为什么？

B. Dialogue II

1. 小夏怎么知道这个星期的天气都不好？

2. 台北夏天的天气很舒服，对不对？

3. 小叶住在什么地方？

4. 台湾什么时候天气最好？

Section Two(True/False)

A. Read the passage and answer the questions.

> 黄先生以前住在台中，台中的天气很好，常常不冷不热，很舒服。黄先生现在在台北工作。台北的冬天天气很糟糕，不但很冷，而且常常下雨。他看报上的天气预报说这个周末台北会下雨，可是台中的天气很好，他想约夏小姐星期天到台中公园走走。

(　) 1. 黄先生在台中住过。

(　) 2. 台中的天气很不错。

(　) 3. 黄先生喜欢台北的冬天。

(　) 4. 这个周末台北的天气比台中好。

(　) 5. 黄先生听朋友说这个周末台北会下雨。

B. Read the passage and answer the questions.

> 叶小姐一个人在加拿大的温哥华工作，他的爸爸妈妈住(zhù: to live)在香港。叶小姐常常去看她的爸爸妈妈，可是她很少夏天回香港，因为香港的夏天又闷又热。叶小姐想请她爸爸妈妈到温哥华来住。可是她的爸爸妈妈已经习惯了香港的天气，而且他们在加拿大没有朋友，所以他们觉得住在那儿没有意思。

(　) 1. 叶小姐的爸爸妈妈常常来加拿大。

(　) 2. 叶小姐常常在夏天回香港。

(　) 3. 叶小姐的爸爸妈妈不觉得香港的夏天太热。

(　) 4. 叶小姐的爸爸妈妈在香港没有朋友。

(　) 5. 叶小姐觉得温哥华夏天的天气比香港好。

(　) 6. 叶小姐的爸爸妈妈觉得住在香港比住在温哥华有意思。

IV. WRITING AND GRAMMAR EXERCISE

Section One

A. Following the model, make sentences using the structure "不但⋯而且⋯".

> Example：漂亮／便宜
>
> ==>这件衬衫不但漂亮，而且便宜。

1. 喜欢听音乐／喜欢看录像：

2. 常常下雨／冷：

3. 贵／颜色不好：

4. 不便宜／不合适：

5. 想去买东西／想去看红叶：

B. Choose the appropriate adverbs to fill in the blanks. (真，太，又，再，更，很)

1. 今天的天气 ＿＿＿＿＿ 热了。

2. 这个录像＿＿＿＿＿好看，我要 ＿＿＿＿＿看一次。

3. 这件衣服＿＿＿＿＿便宜＿＿＿＿＿好看。

4. 上个星期的天气不好，这个星期的天气 ＿＿＿＿＿糟糕。

5. 我觉得写中国字 ＿＿＿＿＿有意思。

6. 他喜欢看电视，但是他＿＿＿＿＿喜欢打球。

7. 他昨天给他弟弟打了一个电话，今天＿＿＿＿＿给他打了一个电话。

8. 这个地方＿＿＿＿＿有意思，我们下个月 ＿＿＿＿＿来一次，好吗？

9. 昨天晚上他不在家，我想他＿＿＿＿＿去看电影了。

10. 第五课的生词＿＿＿＿＿多，可是第六课的生词＿＿＿＿＿多。

C. Rewrite the sentences in each group into a sentence that expresses a comparison with the word 比.

Example: 昨天的天气热。 今天的天气不太热。

    ==> 今天的天气比昨天凉快。

      or: 昨天的天气比今天热。

1. 他这个星期很忙。 他上个星期不太忙。

2. 中文很难，日文更难。

3. 这本书没有意思。那本书更没有意思。

4. 台湾的春天不舒服，秋天舒服。

5. 这个地方的天气很糟糕。那个地方的天气更糟糕。

D.   Write a sentence based on the situation given.

Example: Today's temperatures: Shanghai 95 degrees; Beijing 75 degrees
    ==>今天上海比北京热。
      or：今天北京比上海凉快。

1. Today's temperatures: Hong Kong 90 degrees; Shanghai 85 degrees.

2. Prices for the shirts: yellow ones $16 each; white ones $18 each.

3. Mr. Wang is 5'8"; Mr. Wang's son is 6'2".

4. Little Bai has 5 books; Little Li has 8 books.

5. Chinese is hard; Japanese is harder.

6. Lawyer Zhang is very polite; Lawyer Gao is not too polite.

7. The yellow shirt is not that pretty; the red shirt is very pretty.

8. Beers are expensice; colas are not that expensive.

9. Watching T.V. is not very interesting; going to the movies are really fun.

10. My father's office is big; my mother's office is not that big.

E. Complete the sentences and expand the dialogue.

A: 小谢，明天是星期六，我们去公园看红叶，_____？

B: 好啊，可是我听天气预报说_____。

A: 那我们星期天再出去吧。

B: 可是下个星期天的天气_____。

A: 那怎么办呢？

B: _____。

F. Translate the following sentences into Chinese.

1. This shirt is both nice and cheap. (又...又...)

2. Summer in Taiwan is indeed awful! It is both hot and humid. (又...又...)

3. This shirt is not only very expensive, but also very ugly.
   (不但...而且...)

4. We can not only speak Chinese but also write letters in Chinese.
   (不但...而且..;会)

5. Li You wrote a letter to her mother last week. She wrote her another letter this
   week. (select: 又/再)

6. I called her yesterday, but she wasn't home. I will call her again today.
   (select: 又/再)

7. He went to a movie again last night. (select: 又/再)

8. It was very hot yesterday, but it is even hotter today. (更)

9. English is difficult, but Japanese is more difficult. (更)

10. The weather forecast on the newspaper says that the weather will be better next week. (会)

11. I didn't know how to speak Chinese before, but now I do. (了)

12. The weather is not good today. I'm not going to the park to see the red leaves. (不...了)

13. She was very busy yesterday, but she is no longer busy today. (不...了)

14. Eating Chinese food is more convenient than eating American food. (比)

15. The black shoes are more expensive than the red ones. (比)

Section Two

A. Describe today's weather.

B. Write 10-15 sentences comparing the weather of two of your favorite places. Be sure
   to use these expressions: 不但...而且..., 又...又..., and 比.

C. Give the Chinese version of the passage below:
   I work in Taipei, but both my older brother and older sister are in Shanghai. The
   weather in Shanghai is different from that in Taipei. The summer in Taipei is
   somewhat cooler than Shanghai. Although the winter in Shanghai is colder than
   Taipei, it is a bit more comfortable there. I'd like to go to Shanghai to see my brother
   and sister this fall.

Lesson Eleven   Transportation

I. LISTENING COMPREHENSION

Section One (Listen to the tape for the textbook) (True/False)

A. The Dialogue
(   ) 1. Li You is leaving home for school on 21ˢᵗ..
(   ) 2. Li You should reach the airport no later than 8 p.m..
(   ) 3. Li You decided not to take a taxi because she thought it was too expensive.
(   ) 4. Li You didn't know how to get to the airport by subway.
(   ) 5. In order to get to the airport, Li You can take the subway first, then the bus.
(   ) 6. Li You finally agreed to go to the airport in Wang Peng's car.

B. The Letter
(   ) 1. Wang Peng gave Li You a ride to the airport.
(   ) 2. Li You cannot drive.
(   ) 3. There is bus service but no subway in Li You's hometown.
(   ) 4. Li You was busy visiting old friends.
(   ) 5. Li You felt that everybody drove too slowly.
(   ) 6. Li You enjoyed very much driving on the highway.

Section Two (Listen to the tape for the workbook) (True/False)

A. Dialogue I
(   ) 1. The woman has decided to go home for the summer.
(   ) 2. The man invites the woman to visit his home.
(   ) 3. The man and the woman will drive to the man's home together.
(   ) 4. Airline tickets are on sale now.

B. Dialogue II
(   ) 1. There is no direct bus service between the school and Little Gao's home.
(   ) 2. To get to Little Gao's home by subway, one must first take Red Line, then change to Blue Line.
(   ) 3. The woman decides to go to Little Gao's home by bus.
(   ) 4. There is a bus stop in front of Little Gao's house.

C. Dialogue III
(   ) 1. Old Zhang doesn't know how to drive.
(   ) 2. There is a highway going to the airport.
(   ) 3. Old Zhang will go to the airport with the woman.
(   ) 4. The woman will go to the airport by taxi.

117

II. SPEAKING EXERCISES

Section One (Answer the questions in Chinese based on the texts)

A. The Dialogue
   1. What will Li You do for the winter vacation?
   2. Has Li You made any travel plans for her winter vacation? Please explain.
   3. Please explain how to get to the airport from the school by bus and by subway.
   4. Will Li You go to the airport by taxi? Why?

B. The Letter
   1. How do you express New Year greetings in Chinese?
   2. Why did Li You thank Wang Peng?
   3. What has Li You been doing for the past few days?
   4. Is Li You a good driver? Please explain.

Section Two

A. You need to buy airplane tickets for your winter vacation. Call your travel agent, and reserve a ticket for December 22nd. Tell your travel agent that you prefer a morning flight.

B. What is the best way to get to the airport from your home? Are there any other alternatives?

C. Call your friend and thank him/her for the ride to the airport. Tell him/her what you have been doing since you returned home, and wish your friend a happy New Year.

D. Explain how to get to the airport from your friend's house by referring to the picture below.

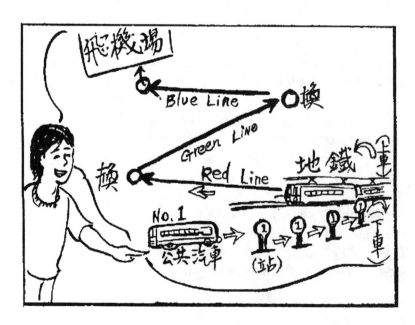

III. READING COMPREHENSION

Section One (Read the text and answer the questions in English.)

A. The Dialogue

    1. 李友的飞机票是哪天的？

    2. 李友坐几点的飞机？

    3. 要是李友坐地铁或者公共汽车，怎么走？

    4. 为什么李友说"太麻烦了"？

    5. 为什么王朋不要李友坐出租汽车？

    6. 你想李友最后怎么去机场？为什麼？

B. The Letter

    1. 为什么李友觉得不好意思？

    2. 李友回家以后，每天都做什么？

    3. 为什么李友开车很紧张？

    4. 为什么李友开车很紧张，可是还是得自己开车？

Section Two

A. Read the following note and answer the questions. (True/False)

小李：

　　请你明天到我家来吃晚饭，因为明天是我的生日。到我家来你可以坐四号公共汽车，也可以坐地铁，都很方便。坐公共汽车慢，可是不用换车。坐地铁快，但是得换车，先坐红线，坐三站，然后换蓝线，坐两站下车就到了。明天见。

　　　　　　　　　　　　　　　　　　　小白

　　　　　　　　　　　　　　　　二月十七日下午三点

（　）1. 小李要请小白吃晚饭。

（　）2. 坐地铁去小白家比坐公共汽车快。

（　）3. 坐地铁或者坐公共汽车都得换车。

（　）4. 小白的生日是二月八号。

（　）5. 坐地铁去小白家一共要坐五站，还得换车。

B. Read the following diary entry and answer the questions. (True/False)

李友的一篇日记

　　今天是我第一次在高速公路上开车。我开车去小王家找他去打球。高速公路上的汽车不但多，而且都开得很快。因为我很紧张，所以迷路 (mílù: to lose one's way) 了。我的车上有电话。我打电话给小王，小王告诉我怎么走。因为我迷路了，所以我很晚才到小王家。

(   ) 1. 李友常常在高速公路上开车。

(   ) 2. 高速公路上的汽车都开得很快。

(   ) 3. 李友开车的时候一点儿都不紧张。

(   ) 4. 李友可以在她的车上打电话。

(   ) 5. 今天的天气很不好，所以李友迷路了。

(   ) 6. 因为李友迷路了，所以小王开车来帮忙。

(   ) 7. 李友去小王家，因为小王请她吃晚饭。

C. Find the corresponding picture for each of the expression below. Put the letter in the parentheses.

1. 出租汽车（   ）   2. 高速公路（   ）   3. 公共汽车（   ）   4. 飞机场（   ）

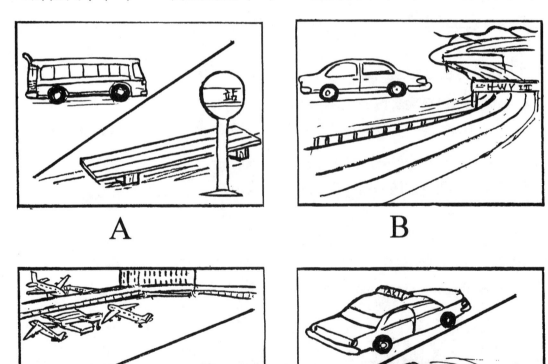

A

B

C

D

IV. WRITING AND GRAMMAR EXERCISES

Section One

A. Write sentences using "先... 再...," based on the information given.

　　Example: 下课以后，他要去图书馆。

　　　　===> 他先上课，再去图书馆。

　　1. 王朋八点吃早饭，九点上电脑课。

　　　　_____。

　　2. 坐公共汽车以前，你得坐地铁。

　　　　_____。

　　3. 我十月五日去日本，十一月六日去英国。

　　　　_____。

　　4. 他吃晚饭以后去看电影。

　　　　_____。

　　5. 李友下午两点去图书馆，四点钟去打球。

　　　　_____。

B. Complete the following sentences with "还是... 吧."

1. 今天的天气真不好，_____。(看电视)

2. 这件衣服太贵，那件虽然颜色不好，可是很便宜。我_____。(买)

3. *A*：我们今天晚上吃中国饭还是吃美国饭？

　　B：_____。

4. *A*：明天又有中国电影，又有音乐会，你说我们去哪儿？

　　B：_____。

C. Fill in the blanks with 或者 or 还是.

    1. 他是中国人 _____ 美国人？

    2. 到你家去，坐地铁方便 _____ 坐公共汽车方便？

    3. 你想买红色的，黄色的，_____ 绿色的？

    4. 今天晚上我想在家看书 _____看电视。

    5. 我想要一杯咖啡_____ 一瓶可乐。

D. Change the following sentences into the "topic-comment" structure.

    Example： 她很喜欢那件衬衫。

        ===> 那件衬衫她很喜欢。

    1. 我复习了昨天的语法。

    _____ 。

    2. 你买飞机票了吗？

    _____ 。

    3. 我们都很喜欢喝中国茶。

    _____ 。

    4. 我很不习惯这儿的天气。

    _____ 。

    5. 真不好意思让你花钱。

    _____ 。

E. Translate the following sentences into Chinese.

    1. It is raining. You had better stay home and watch video tapes. (还是...吧)

    2. *A:* Should I take the bus or the subway to go to the airport?

       B: You can go to the airport either by bus or by subway.

    3. You drive me to the airport tomorrow, can you?.

    4. I listen to the tapes every morning. (每...都)

    5. I have seen <u>that Chinese movie.</u>(topic-comment)

    6. Let's learn the pronunciation before we learn the characters. (先...再...)

    7. First, you take the bus, then change to subway. Finally you have to take a taxi.
       (先...再...，最后...)

    8. It's too much trouble to write him a letter. Let's call him instead. (还是)

    9. You can go to the airport by subway. First, you take the green line, and then
       you change to the blue line.

Section Two

A. Describe your experiences driving or traveling on the highway.

B. Describe in detail how to get to the airport from your school.

C. Translate the following passage into Chinese.
The winter vacation starts next week. In the winter vacation I will go home to see my parents. My dad bought me a plane ticket. (会) My mom called me yesterday. She told me that she had bought me three new shirts, a blue one, a red one, and a green one. I don't know whether I will like those colors or not.(V + 不 +V) Dad will drive to the airport, and my younger brother will go with him. I will see them at the airport. I talked to Mom on the phone in Chinese. (用 . . . V. . .) She said that my Chinese had improved. I was very happy.